GREAT
BUILDING
FEATS

THE
HOOVER
DAM

LESLEY A. DuTEMPLE

Lerner Publications Company
Minneapolis

For Richard Coates Lowrie (1905–1956)
A New York boy who became one of the "dam builders of the
West," chief engineer for Morrison-Knudsen, and the father-in-law I
never knew

Lerner Publications Company
A division of Lerner Publishing Group
241 First Avenue North
Minneapolis, MN 55401 U.S.A.

Website address: www.lernerbooks.com

Library of Congress Cataloging-in-Publication Data

DuTemple, Lesley A.
      The Hoover Dam / by Lesley A. Du Temple.
          p.   cm. — (Great building feats)
      Includes bibliographical references and index.
      Contents: A wild river (to 1920)—Boulder or Black? (1919–1931)—Getting ready to build
a dam (1931)—Moving the Colorado River (1931–1932)—Model city and more
(1931–1932)—The dam goes up (1933–1934)—Taming the Colorado? (1935 to modern
times)
      ISBN: 0–8225–4691–4 (lib. bdg. : alk. paper)
      1. Hoover Dam (Ariz. and Nev.)—History—Juvenile literature. 2. Dams—Colorado River
(Colo.–Mexico)—Design and construction—Juvenile literature. [1. Hoover Dam (Ariz. and
Nev.)] I. Title. II. Series.
TC557.5.H6 D88 2003
627'.82'0979313—dc21   2002013951

Manufactured in the United States of America
1 2 3 4 5 6 – JR – 08 07 06 05 04 03

CONTENTS

ABOUT *GREAT BUILDING FEATS* **4**

Chapter One: A WILD RIVER **8**

Chapter Two: BOULDER OR BLACK? **18**

Chapter Three: GETTING READY TO BUILD A DAM **30**

Chapter Four: MOVING THE COLORADO RIVER **40**

Chapter Five: MODEL CITY AND MORE **56**

Chapter Six: THE DAM GOES UP **70**

Chapter Seven: TAMING THE COLORADO? **80**

A TIMELINE OF THE HOOVER DAM **90**

SOURCE NOTES **92**

SELECTED BIBLIOGRAPHY **92**

FURTHER READING AND WEBSITES **93**

INDEX **94**

ABOUT GREAT BUILDING FEATS

HUMANS HAVE LONG SOUGHT to make their mark on the world. From the ancient Great Wall of China to the ultramodern Channel Tunnel linking Great Britain and France, grand structures reveal how people have tried to express themselves and better their lives.

Great structures have served a number of purposes. Sometimes they met a practical need. For example, the New York subway system made getting around a huge city easier. Other structures reflected spiritual beliefs. The Pantheon in Rome, Italy, was created as a temple to Roman gods and later became a Catholic church. Sometimes we can only guess at the story behind a structure. The purpose of Stonehenge in England eludes us, and perhaps it always will.

This book is one in a series called Great Building Feats. Each book in the series takes a close look at some of the most amazing

Above, participants on a hard hat tour of Hoover Dam are awed by its size. *Right,* Hoover Dam creates a deep lake upstream of it.

building feats around the world. Each of them posed a unique set of engineering and geographical problems. In many cases, these problems seemed nearly insurmountable when construction began.

More than a compilation of facts, the Great Building Feats series not only describes how each structure was built but also why. Each project called forth the best minds of its time. Many people invested their all in the outcome. Their lives are as much a part of the structure as the earth and stone used in its construction.

Finally, each structure in the Great Building Feats series remains a dynamic feature of the modern world, still amazing users and viewers as well as historians.

THE HOOVER DAM

One of the most daunting canyons in the world lies 30 miles (48 kilometers) south of Las Vegas, Nevada. Carved out by the mighty Colorado River, Black Canyon cuts a 1,200-foot (366-meter) deep gash in the desert landscape. Deep in the canyon, as well as on the plain above, weather conditions fluctuate wildly.

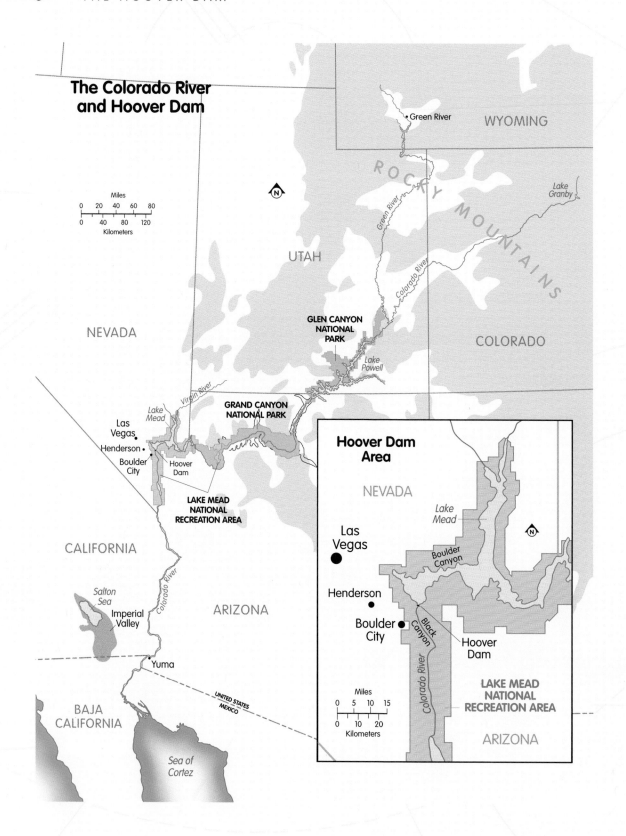

The Colorado River and Hoover Dam

Miles
0 20 40 60 80

0 40 80 120
Kilometers

WYOMING

• Green River

R O C K Y   M O U N T A I N S

Lake Granby

UTAH

NEVADA

Green River

Colorado River

GLEN CANYON NATIONAL PARK

COLORADO

Lake Powell

Virgin River

Lake Mead

GRAND CANYON NATIONAL PARK

Las Vegas •
Henderson •
Boulder City •

Hoover Dam

LAKE MEAD NATIONAL RECREATION AREA

CALIFORNIA

Salton Sea

Imperial Valley

Colorado River

ARIZONA

Yuma

UNITED STATES
MEXICO

BAJA CALIFORNIA

Sea of Cortez

Hoover Dam Area

NEVADA

Lake Mead

Boulder Canyon

Las Vegas
●

Henderson
●

Boulder City
●

Black Canyon

Hoover Dam

Colorado River

LAKE MEAD NATIONAL RECREATION AREA

ARIZONA

Miles
0 5 10 15

0 10 20
Kilometers

From May through September, temperatures reach 130 degrees Fahrenheit (54 degrees Celsius). Under a searing sun, rocks become too hot to touch. From December until March, icy winds swirl clouds of dust into the canyon and send sheets of freezing rain scudding across the barren plain above. Few animals live in these conditions. Even reptiles avoid Black Canyon.

Yet from 1931 through 1935, more than five thousand men lived and worked in Black Canyon. Twenty-four hours a day, seven days a week—regardless of the weather—these men toiled ceaselessly.

They were building a dam to harness the Colorado River, one of the roughest rivers in the world. For centuries the Colorado River was considered wild and impassable. After white men first explored the area, it took more than three hundred years to get it mapped because no one could successfully travel the entire river by boat.

In the end, the Colorado River was conquered, but at a terrible cost. Officially ninety-six workers died during the construction of Hoover Dam. This number reflects only those killed in accidents at the job site, however. Unofficially the number is much higher. During one four-week period in 1931, fourteen workers died of heatstroke at the workers' camp. Many tunnel workers were sent to the hospital, where their cause of death was listed as "pneumonia." As was later shown, they died of carbon monoxide poisoning, the consequence of using gasoline-powered vehicles in the closed tunnels. The deaths of these people and many others are not reflected in the official ninety-six total. No one will ever know the true human cost, since accurate records were not kept.

By harnessing the power of the Colorado River to control its raging floods and to provide hydroelectric energy, Hoover Dam paved the way for the development of the West. Los Angeles, Phoenix, and Las Vegas grew from small desert towns, struggling to meet their water and power needs, into sprawling centers of urban growth, with lush lawns and golf courses.

But it very nearly didn't happen. The story of Hoover Dam is a story of hardship and perseverance. It is the story of a great building feat.

Chapter One
A WILD RIVER

(Before 1920)

Above, melting snow rushes down the slopes of the Rocky Mountains to the Colorado River.
Right, the Colorado River flows through the Grand Canyon before it reaches Hoover Dam.

EACH SPRING IN THE TOWERING peaks of the Rocky Mountains in Wyoming, Colorado, and Utah, melting snow dribbles through rocky canyons and across marshy alpine meadows. Moving ever downward, the trickles gather and swell into icy streams. These small streams are the start of the mighty Colorado River, which continues southwest through Colorado and the high desert of Utah.

In springtime, the Colorado races through narrow canyons, carrying tens of thousands of cubic feet of water. Even in winter, it can flood without warning, rising 17 feet (5 m) in an hour.

Leaving Utah, the river slashes through the Grand Canyon in northern Arizona. Then it travels westward. By the time it enters Black Canyon, just south of Las Vegas, Nevada, the Colorado has become a raging torrent. Its waters can rush by at the speed of 175 feet (53 m) per second or more.

The river continues south, picking up its last major source of water from the Gila River in Arizona. From there, it follows the Arizona-California border. The Colorado's long journey, 1,430 miles (2,300 km), ends in Mexico, 50 miles

(80 km) south of the United States-Mexico border. There, it sprawls into a huge tidal delta (where river sediment collects at the mouth of a river) at the head of the Gulf of California in the Pacific Ocean. By the end of its journey, the Colorado has gathered water in Wyoming, Utah, Colorado, Nevada, New Mexico, and Arizona. The river has carved this path for millions of years.

A PATHWAY TO GOLD?

Although the water in the Colorado originates in the snowy mountains of the north, much of the river's journey takes it through desert regions. The river is wild, but it is also a boon to a region that receives little rain.

For centuries the Colorado supported several Native American desert cultures. Archaeologists think these tribes used the river primarily for irrigation. It was too unreliable and dangerous to use for transportation.

The river was first seen by Europeans in 1540. Spanish explorers traveling north from Mexico tried to navigate the river in search of gold and new territories. The swift current and roiling rapids hurled their boats against jagged rocks. The narrow, towering canyons proved impassable. It wasn't until 330 years later that the Colorado River was navigated and mapped.

NAVIGATING THE UNNAVIGABLE

After the Mexican-American War ended in 1848, the territories of California, Arizona, and New Mexico became part of the United States. The federal government in Washington, D.C., began to think seriously about the Colorado River, which ran through these new territories. The government was interested in the river's commercial possibilities. In the

Spanish conquistadors (explorers) soon gave up their hopes that the Colorado River would lead them to gold.

developed regions farther east, the Mississippi River was a vital channel of commerce. The ability to use the Colorado River to transport goods would benefit the developing western region.

In 1857 the U.S. War Department ordered Lieutenant Joseph Ives to navigate up the Colorado River in *The Explorer*, a 58-foot (18 m) iron-hulled steamboat. In 1858, starting from Yuma, Arizona, Ives and his crew of twenty-four headed north. A clumsy, heavy boat, *The Explorer* ran aground on a sandbar only 1 mile (1.6 km) upstream. It took more than five hours to get it floating again. This troublesome departure proved only the beginning of the expedition's problems. Sandbars and accidents plagued Ives throughout the trip.

Still, by March 1858, he had managed to travel 400 miles (644 km) upstream and to make it to the mouth of Black Canyon. There, *The Explorer* struck a rock and suffered serious damage. While repairs were being made, Ives and two crew members took a small wooden boat farther upstream. They made it through Black Canyon and continued 3 miles (5 km) beyond it before turning back.

In his report to the War Department in Washington, D.C., Ives noted that the Colorado River could be used, with caution, to transport supplies as far north as Black Canyon. Beyond that, he said, "Ours was the first, and will doubtless be the last, party of whites to visit this profitless locality. It seems intended by Nature that the Colorado River, along with the greater portion of its lonely and majestic way, shall be forever unvisited and undisturbed."

> "Ours was the first, and will doubtless be the last, party of whites to visit this profitless locality."
>
> —Lieutenant Joseph Ives

JOHN WESLEY POWELL AND THE COLORADO

The federal government abandoned the idea of using the Colorado River for navigation and commerce. But it was still a magnet for explorers and adventurers. The wild rapids attracted thrill seekers, while continuing to defeat anyone attempting to run its full course—until John Wesley Powell decided to tackle the river.

Powell, a one-armed Civil War veteran, was a scientist, geologist, teacher, and government explorer. He was also an intrepid adventurer. Ever since European explorers had first seen the Colorado, there had been stories of tremendous waterfalls, swirling rapids, and whirlpools that sucked boats under. Powell was determined to learn the truth. In May 1869, he and nine other men put into the river with four wooden boats at Green River, Wyoming. They would travel on the Green River until it joined the Colorado in Utah.

Even on the Green River, the rapids were foaming and treacherous. One of the boats was destroyed almost immediately. By July they had reached the point of no return—the section of the Colorado leading into Grand, Boulder, and Black Canyons. Here they faced steep canyon walls and beyond them, the desert. One of Powell's men was so disheartened by what they'd already experienced that he left the expedition there.

On August 28, 1869, after weeks of fighting the Grand Canyon's worst rapids, three more members of Powell's expedition left. They were determined to get off the relentless river. The departing expedition members somehow managed to climb out of the Grand Canyon, only to be killed by Paiute Indians. Powell and his remaining five men continued on. Another boat struck a rock and was destroyed.

Above, John Wesley Powell
Below, Powell, his crew, and well-wishers gather at the Green River.

Terrified but determined, all six men continued in only two boats.

On August 30, 1869, more than three months after they had set off from Green River, Wyoming, Powell's expedition passed the place where the Virgin River entered the Colorado in Nevada. Local fishermen standing on the bank waved at them. They had made it through the previously impassable sections of the river.

Powell's successful navigation of the Colorado River produced a flurry of activity in the region. Other explorers followed, and Powell even returned in 1871 to do a survey of the entire river. The river had been mapped, but it was still rough and untamed. Almost another twenty years passed before anyone else was able to duplicate his feat. In his report, Powell agreed with Ives that the area was a "profitless locality."

John K. Hillers took this photo of the Grand Canyon while working with Powell in the 1870s.

THE COST OF A BLOOMING DESERT

In the early 1900s, the Colorado River was still rough, muddy, and virtually unnavigable. It still flowed through a barren wasteland, but it held a lot of water between its banks. Ever since the California gold rush of the mid-1800s, people had been moving to the West to mine for gold or to provide goods and services to miners. All of them needed water.

These settlers began to view the Colorado the way Native Americans had. Native Americans had taken advantage of the river's flooding, planting crops in the rich silt when the waters receded. If the Colorado couldn't be used for commerce, its waters could be used to irrigate crops and to build towns and farming communities in the desert.

In 1901 a private development company built a canal 100 yards (90 m) north of the Mexican border. Its purpose was to divert most of the water of the Colorado River to the Imperial Valley in California. The company had already sold land in the Imperial Valley to would-be farmers. All of them had bought the parched desert land based on the promise of water.

The Imperial Valley is a 2,000-square-mile (5,180-sq.-km) area that lies to the west of the Colorado River. Its eastern rim is approximately 100 feet (30 m) above sea level. But the center of the valley, known as the Salton Sink, is 230 feet (70 m) below sea level. The region was once an ancient lake. The water in the lake had evaporated over a period of thousands of years as the southwest became hotter.

When the canal opened, the transformation was amazing. By 1904 seven thousand people lived in the once desolate valley. Agriculture was booming. Farmers grew vegetables and fruits. They raised poultry and grazed more than ten thousand head of cattle on irrigated pastureland. But this huge oasis in the California desert was threatened when the development company ran into financial difficulties.

Every spring, floodwaters rushed down the river, loaded with silt—the soil, sand, and gravel it picked up as it raced through the canyons. Tons of this silt were deposited when the river slowed down in its lower reaches—just where the canal had been built. Because the private development company was in financial trouble, it didn't maintain the canal, which gradually filled up with the river silt.

In the spring of 1905, a series of devastating floods wiped out the control gates that regulated the flow of river water going into the Imperial Valley. The river swiftly carved the small canal into a half-mile-wide (800-m) channel.

More floods hit the river. By November 1905, the Colorado River was flowing unchecked through the canal and roaring into the Imperial Valley. The great force of the water, and the depth of the Salton Sink compared to the surrounding area, forced the river to abandon its original southward course to the Pacific Ocean. It moved entirely into the Imperial Valley.

Within days the Salton Sink became the Salton Sea, a 150-square-mile (389-sq.-km) lake, 60 feet (18 m) deep. Worst of all was the "cutback" phenomenon. The river created a waterfall at the place it poured into the bottom of the sink. But the sandy soil at the lip of the falls was too loose to support the volume of water running over it. The waterfall kept cutting back through the sand toward the river at the rate of 1 mile (1.6 km) per day. What had started off as a relatively small waterfall quickly turned into a thunderous torrent more than 100 feet (30 m) high.

Left, the Imperial Valley produced a variety of crops, including canteloupe, after the canal brought Colorado River water to the area. *Above*, massive flooding destroyed much of the valley in the early 1900s.

Engineers surveyed the ever-increasing disaster. They realized that if the cutback reached the original canal intake, the waterfall would be almost 300 feet (91 m) high. The Colorado River would never be able to return to the Pacific Ocean. Geologists also predicted that the river wouldn't stop there. It would continue cutting back, carving out a canyon 1 mile (1.6 km) deep and several hundred miles long. It would destroy Yuma, Arizona, and flood all of southwestern Arizona and southern California.

In the four years since the canal had opened, people had forgotten how powerful the Colorado River could be. After the canal burst, people realized that the Colorado River had to be returned to its natural channel, no matter what the cost. It would be unthinkable to turn Arizona and southern California into an inland sea.

PUTTING THE COLORADO BACK

The canal's failing development company had turned over all its property to the Southern Pacific Railroad before the river had destroyed the control gate. President Theodore Roosevelt personally appealed to Edward H. Harriman, the owner of the Southern Pacific Railroad, to stop the rampaging river.

Harriman ordered every Southern Pacific freight train in the Southwest to haul rocks and lumber to the site. The railroad erected an enormous bridge across the intake channel, and trains began dumping rock into the torrent. On February 10, 1907, the Colorado River was finally diverted from the Imperial Valley and pushed back into its original channel. It took two years and more than $3 million to put the river back in its bed and return its flow to the Pacific Ocean.

LETTING GO OF THE DREAM

The Imperial Valley was devastated, but it was hard to abandon the memory of a fertile, blooming desert. For the next ten years, various private canals were built to divert the Colorado River into the desert. The river wiped them all out, usually with a devastating spring flood.

Many people, especially those living in the Imperial Valley, felt that a large canal, built and maintained by the government, was needed. It was the only way to manage the Colorado River and make the desert bloom. Others, especially Arthur Powell Davis, director of the U.S. Bureau of Reclamation (the government agency primarily responsible for water and land use), felt differently. Davis thought canals were useful but that a dam on the Colorado would be even better.

Southern Pacific Railroad cars dumped rocks into the canal to force the Colorado River back into its original bed, or path.

Chapter Two
BOULDER OR BLACK?
(1919–1931)

AS THE NEPHEW OF JOHN Wesley Powell, Arthur Powell Davis had grown up on the stories of the daring exploits of his mother's brother. He loved the Colorado River and the desert regions surrounding it. He had spent years tramping through the area of rivers and streams that drained into the Colorado. No one knew the Colorado River Basin, the region through which it flowed, better than Arthur Powell Davis. And no one believed in its potential as strongly as Davis did.

When a congressional bill for a canal in the Imperial Valley was defeated in 1919, it was largely due to the efforts of Davis. He opposed the All-American Canal Bill because he thought it was inadequate. He thought a network of dams was needed to control the Colorado. Without dams, the unpredictable Colorado would continue to break through the floodgates of any canal built.

The first dam would be the most important, Davis thought. It would also have to be the largest because, at first, it would have to control the entire Colorado River by itself.

WHERE SHOULD THE DAM BE BUILT?

Agreeing with Davis that dams were needed to control the Colorado, the government launched an intensive study of the river. Geologists (scientists

Canyon surveyors had to climb to dangerous heights with bulky equipment to do their job.

who study rock formations) and hydrologists (scientists who study water and its properties) pored over the Colorado River Basin. They focused on the stretches of river along the Nevada-Arizona border.

The government team considered three factors in searching for a dam site. The first was the geology of the site. Because the dam would anchor into the canyon walls, the rocks would have to be strong. Second, the area would have to be able to store huge amounts of water and silt because the dam would create a large reservoir (lake) behind it. Third, the site needed to be near a major railway. Supplies and equipment would have to be shipped in, and the government didn't want to build new rail lines as well as a new dam.

In addition, the government wanted a site near a populated region. Dams create hydropower, which can be used to generate electricity. The government hoped to pay for the cost of the new dam by selling its hydropower to the fast-growing cities in southern California. So, finding a site near this booming region was critical.

In 1922 the results of this initial government dam study were published in the Fall-Davis Report. The document was hundreds of pages long, but most people were only interested in a small paragraph on page twenty-one. There it recommended that the United States construct, with government funds, a huge dam "at or near Boulder Canyon."

The choice had been narrowed down to two sites—Boulder Canyon and Black Canyon. Only 20 miles (32 km) apart, both canyons were high and narrow and looked good for a dam. Because Davis thought Boulder Canyon was more suitable, the Colorado River dam project was soon called the Boulder Dam Project, or the Boulder Canyon Dam.

THE BOULDER DAM . . . IN BLACK CANYON

Another team of government surveyors and scientists was sent to both canyons. Their first task was to choose one canyon. Next, they would have to pick the exact spot for a dam. Once the precise spot was picked, engineers could design the structure and figure out the cost. Congress would then be able to approve and set aside the funds.

The survey team started at Boulder Canyon to try to determine the depth, strength, and composition of the canyon's granite walls. The whole region was harsh and forbidding. The walls of Boulder Canyon were 1,200 feet (366 m) high, rising directly out of the water. The fifty-eight men on the survey team crammed into twenty-eight small tents, clustered on a narrow graveled beach just upstream from Boulder Canyon.

The men rode drilling barges to the sites. There they drilled core samples from the bottom of the river to find the depth of the silt and the strength of the underlying rock, since the dam needed to rest on solid rock. The work was backbreaking and dangerous. The river current swirled swiftly and unevenly, making it impossible to anchor the

Drilling crews tested the depth of silt and the strength of the underlying rock in both Boulder Canyon and Black Canyon from a barge such as this one.

barges. To hold the barges steady, the men drove iron rings into the canyon walls and tethered the boats to them with steel cables. Despite this, one of the barges tore loose, and a driller was killed. The samples indicated that Boulder Canyon was not a suitable location for a dam, so the survey team moved on to Black Canyon.

Construction engineer Walker Young took this photograph of Black Canyon in 1932. The photo looks upstream at the dam site before construction began.

Weather conditions and geological formations in Black Canyon were just as harsh. Shortly after the crew set up camp on a small rocky beach, a strong wind roared down the canyon and blew away the entire campsite—twenty-eight tents, pots, pans, and equipment. Everything had to be shipped in and set up again, delaying work for more than a week.

Black Canyon, particularly the lower end of it, turned out to be a better location. It had less silt and debris to excavate from the riverbed, and the foundation rock was more stable than at Boulder Canyon.

WHAT'S IN A NAME?

Starting with Arthur Powell Davis's suggestion that Boulder Canyon would be the best spot for a dam, the name of the world's largest dam changed names six times. After Boulder Canyon Dam, it became the Black Canyon Dam. Then it became the Boulder Canyon Project. On September 17, 1930, it was officially named Hoover Dam. When President Herbert Hoover failed to win reelection, his successor, President Franklin D. Roosevelt, renamed it Boulder Dam in his 1935 dedication speech. In 1947 the dam's name was, again and finally, officially changed back to Hoover Dam.

A DAM TO HOLD
BACK THE COLORADO RIVER

With the site at the lower end of Black Canyon pinpointed, engineers began working on the structural design for the "Boulder Dam." Because Davis originally suggested a Boulder Canyon site, government reports and newspapers continued to call the project the Boulder Dam. Even after the dam was officially named Hoover Dam on September 17, 1930, in honor of President Herbert Hoover, the name Boulder Dam continued to stick.

Led by chief engineer Raymond Walter and chief design engineer Jack Savage, the Bureau of Reclamation researched all possible dam designs for what would become the largest dam in the world. Walter and Savage decided that only one design would be strong enough to hold back the Colorado River. An arched-gravity design would get its strength from the arched shape of the dam. An arch is one of the best ways to spread pressure, or force, evenly throughout a structure. The top of the arch absorbs the greatest pressure. From there, the pressure moves out along the curves of the arch to the edges. "Arched-gravity" means that gravity would also transmit the force downward into the earth.

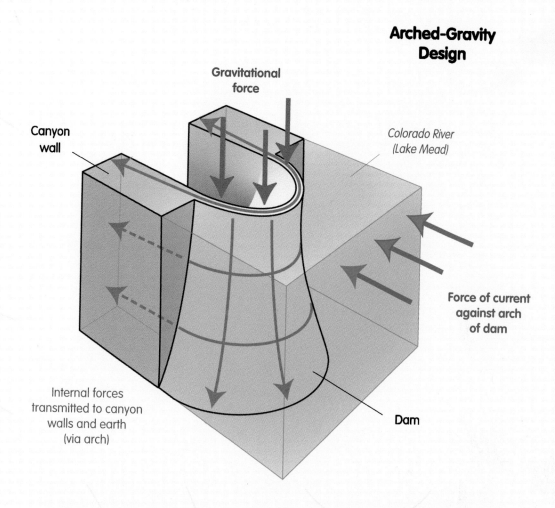

Arched-Gravity Design

Gravitational force

Canyon wall

Colorado River (Lake Mead)

Force of current against arch of dam

Internal forces transmitted to canyon walls and earth (via arch)

Dam

The curve of the arch would face the flow of the Colorado River. When the raging current hit the dam, the arch design would transmit the force across the face of the dam and into the canyon walls, where the sides of the dam would be anchored. The canyon walls would absorb more pressure than the dam itself.

The dam would be made of concrete, a mixture of gravel, cement, and water that hardens as it dries. Concrete is strongest under compression—the harder and tighter it's packed, the stronger it is. The Hoover Dam arch would also be thick at the bottom and thin at the top, resembling a giant "C" wedged between the walls of the canyon. More than thirty engineering plans, varying in height, thickness, and materials, were tested and discarded. The final dimensions would be 660 feet (201 m) thick at the base, and 45 feet (14 m) thick at the top. It would be 1,282 feet (391 m) wide and tower 726 feet (221 m) —as tall as a sixty-story office building.

A gravel-processing plant and two concrete mixing facilities would have to be built at the site. It wasn't feasible to transport that much gravel and concrete over long distances. The gravel-processing plant became the largest in the United States, and it produced only for the dam.

MORE THAN JUST A WALL OF CONCRETE

The enormous concrete face of the dam would be its most obvious feature, and its gravel-processing plant and concrete-mixing facilities were perhaps the most indispensible. But there was a lot more to build than just a concrete obstacle in the middle of a scorching desert canyon. In addition to the dam, diversion tunnels, intake towers, concrete spillways, a power station, a railway, and even a city to house the workers would have to be constructed.

The basic plans for Hoover Dam called for four concrete-lined diversion tunnels, two on the Nevada side of the canyon and two on the Arizona side. Each tunnel would run about three-quarters of a mile (1.2

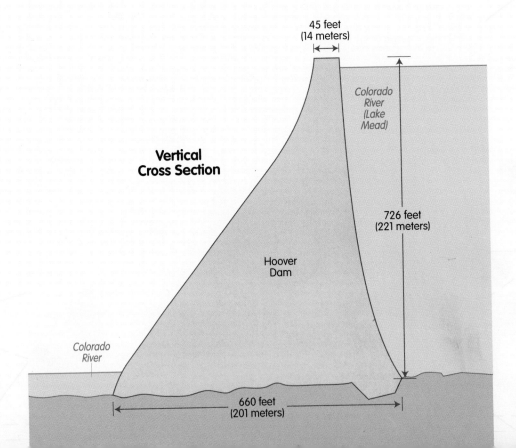

45 feet
(14 meters)

Colorado
River
(Lake
Mead)

**Vertical
Cross Section**

726 feet
(221 meters)

Hoover
Dam

Colorado
River

660 feet
(201 meters)

km) through the cliffs. After the tunnels were drilled, two earth cofferdams (watertight structures to prevent the river water from flowing in) would be built. One would be just below the tunnel entrance and one just above the tunnel outlets.

The cofferdam below the tunnel entrances, or intakes, would force the river into the four tunnels. When it emerged, nearly 1 mile (1.6 km) down the canyon, the cofferdam just above the outlets would keep water from backwashing into the dam construction area. The tunnels and cofferdams would give the workers about 1 mile (1.6 km) of dry riverbed in which to construct the dam.

Since the government planned to sell hydropower, a massive power plant also had to be built. Four giant intake towers, 395 feet (120 m) high, would be built in the reservoir created just behind the dam. The intake towers would take up water from the reservoir created by the dam and send it to the generators in the power plant to produce electricity. Since

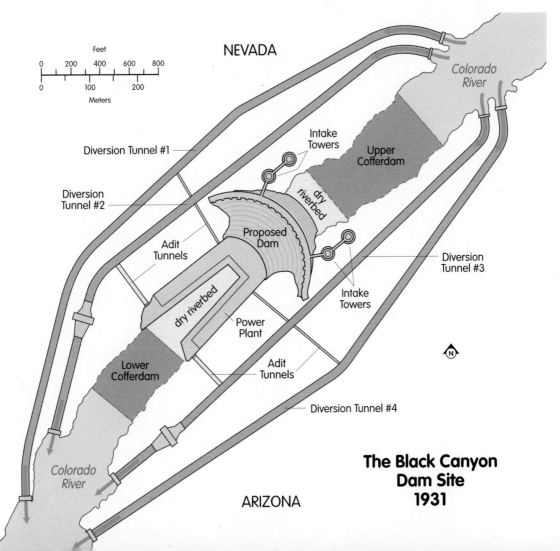

Feet
0 200 400 600 800

0 100 200
Meters

NEVADA

Colorado River

Diversion Tunnel #1

Diversion Tunnel #2

Intake Towers

Upper Cofferdam

dry riverbed

Adit Tunnels

Proposed Dam

Diversion Tunnel #3

Intake Towers

Power Plant

dry riverbed

Lower Cofferdam

Adit Tunnels

Diversion Tunnel #4

Colorado River

ARIZONA

The Black Canyon Dam Site 1931

the site was 30 miles (48 km) from the nearest town, Las Vegas, a rail system and highway would have to be built to the Black Canyon area.

Then there were the workers. More than five thousand workers would be needed to build the dam. They couldn't all just camp out in the harsh environment of the desert. The projected plans called for an entire city to be built, 7 miles (11 km) from the site. It would contain houses, stores, dormitories, a recreation center, and a mess hall.

BIDDING ON THE DAM

Every part of the project had to be designed, budgeted, and accounted for so Congress could allocate the funds. On January 10, 1931, Congress released the specifications for Hoover Dam to the public and asked for

THE COLORADO RIVER COMPACT

Hoover Dam would change the way water moved in the West, so government officials had to figure out how the water in the Colorado River would be divided. Even though the river didn't run through California, California thought it should get the most water. Residents of Arizona were vehemently opposed to Californians getting more water than they did. People in Utah, Colorado, and Wyoming thought they should get a large portion of it since most of the water came from their states.

President Warren Harding put his secretary of commerce, Herbert Hoover, in charge of the negotiations. Hoover avoided the problem of a state-by-state allocation by breaking the Colorado River basin into two divisions. The upper division included Utah, Wyoming, Colorado, and New Mexico, and the lower division included Arizona, California, and Nevada. Actual state allocations would be determined later on.

All the states ratified (approved) the compact, or agreement, except Arizona. The compact still went into effect because one clause stated that it would be binding if six of seven states ratified it. Arizona fought the compact in the courts but lost. By June 25, 1929, the final details of the Colorado River Compact were worked out, and funding for the dam was approved.

bids. Although the government created the design and put up the money, private construction companies would bid for the right to build the dam. For five dollars, any private construction company could obtain a copy of the plans. All bids had to be submitted by March 4, 1931. Whoever built Hoover Dam would have seven years to do it. Deadlines were set for the completion of various phases of the work, with penalties for deadlines not met.

To discourage frivolous bids, the government required that every bid had to be accompanied by a $2 million refundable deposit. The bid winner would have to deposit an additional $5 million with the government.

The dam designers gave the government an estimate of $48, 866,955 as the cost of constructing the dam. The contract for the dam's construction would be the largest ever awarded by the government.

When private companies bid on a government project, they aren't told the government's estimated cost. They have to look at the plans and specifications, then figure out how much it will cost them to fulfill the requirements. The bidder that comes closest to the undisclosed estimate usually gets the project.

SIX COMPANIES, INCORPORATED

In 1931 the United States was in the depths of the Great Depression. Banks had closed, companies had gone bankrupt, and millions of people were unemployed. For many construction companies, the opportunity to build part of the world's largest dam was extremely welcome. Their employees would be working, and the companies would be making money again. Scores of private construction companies sent for the plans. Everybody was very enthusiastic.

When they looked closely at what was required, however, their enthusiasm waned. No single construction company in the world could build Hoover Dam. The project was too huge. The requirement that the company put up $2 million, with a potential for another $5 million, was another limiting factor. In the midst of the Great Depression, few companies—even successful ones—could raise that much money.

The only way to build the dam was for companies to form partnerships. During the spring of 1931, two of the largest dam-building construction companies in the West, Utah Construction and Morrison-Knudsen, did just that. Before they could bid on the project, Utah Construction and Morrison-

Knudsen had to add still more partners—J. F. Shea, Pacific Bridge, MacDonald & Kahn, and Bechtel-Kaiser-Warren Brothers.

Called Six Companies, Incorporated, the group put together a bid and submitted it to the government. Even with six large, successful companies banding together, it was still difficult to come up with the initial money required. To get $2 million and have another $5 million lined up, the group pledged to the bank 25,000 cattle and 30,000 sheep, among other assets.

AND THE WINNER IS . . .

On the morning of March 4, 1931, the Denver office of the U. S. Bureau of Reclamation was packed with people. Cigar smoke filled the air, newspaper reporters spilled out into the corridors, and contractors waited nervously. Although many companies had

been interested in bidding on the project, only five bids had been submitted.

Raymond Walter, chief engineer of the Bureau of Reclamation, spread the sealed envelopes containing the bids on a table at the front of the room. Neither of the first two bids was accompanied by the required $2 million. The next two bids were in order. One was for $53.9 million and the other was for $58.6 million. Only the bid from Six Companies remained. Walter opened the last envelope and read, "Six Companies, Incorporated, San Francisco, California, $48,890,955." Their bid was only $24,000 more than the government's estimated cost of the project.

Shouts erupted from the crowd and flashbulbs popped. Newspaper reporters rushed from the room to file their reports. Six Companies had won the right to build the biggest dam in the world.

Officials of the Bureau of Reclamation and Six Companies gathered in Boulder City, Nevada, include Frank Crowe, superintendent of construction, *second from right*; and Walker Young, a Bureau of Reclamation construction engineer, *far right.*

Chapter Three
GETTING READY TO BUILD A DAM
(1931)

ON THE MORNING OF MARCH 11, 1931, a crowd of dignitaries, politicians, and newspaper reporters waited anxiously as a smoke-belching, black locomotive chugged into the dusty Las Vegas train station. The train ground to a halt with an ear-splitting screech. The crowd on the platform surged forward, peering into the windows. Frank Crowe, the man in charge of building Hoover Dam, was on that train, and everyone wanted to meet him.

The dam builders of the West were a small, almost elite, fraternity. Only a handful of private companies built dams, so the engineers and experienced workers traveled from site to site

The Las Vegas railroad depot was draped in patriotic colors to welcome the dam construction managers.

following the work. Although the engineers were well educated, they were a rough-and-tumble lot who preferred the wide-open spaces of the West to desk jobs in the East.

Frank Crowe was already a legend within this group. With an engineering degree from the University of Maine, he was not only well educated but also smart and creative. He had an uncanny ability to solve tough engineering problems in unique ways. His specialties were high concrete dams and cable transportation systems. Only in his forties, he had already built six dams. He finished all of them on time and under budget, which made employers love him. And as a supervisor he was fair, so field-workers loved him too.

Crowe was superintendent of construction for Morrison-Knudsen. Aside from the Six Companies connection, Morrison-Knudsen and Utah Construction also had a separate partnership, and Frank Crowe was in charge of construction for that enterprise, too.

Crowe's reputation was the main reason Morrison-Knudsen and Utah Construction had been able to find other partners, form Six Companies, and win the government bid. Crowe had avidly followed the progress of the Boulder Canyon Project. His skills and judgment were so respected that Arthur Powell Davis had met with him several times during the course of government planning and even asked him to help to work up a budget for the project.

> "I was wild to build. . . . the biggest dam ever built by anyone anywhere."
>
> —Frank Crowe

Crowe considered his previous dam-building experience just a warm-up for this one massive project. As he said years later, "I was wild to build this dam. I had spent my life in the river bottoms, and [Hoover Dam] meant a wonderful climax—the biggest dam ever built by anyone anywhere."

Other top engineers had said that the huge dimensions made the dam impossible to build. They said the enormous reservoir created by the dam would put too much pressure on the earth. This would cause catastrophic earthquakes that would crack the concrete in the dam. The dam would burst and flood everything in its path including southern California. As he stepped from the train, Frank Crowe knew it was up to him to prove them wrong.

TOO MANY WORKERS, NOT ENOUGH JOBS

Since late 1930, when construction of the dam had been officially announced, unemployed workers and their families had been pouring into Las Vegas. Because of the Great Depression, millions of people were out of work. They did whatever they could to squeak by.

THE GREAT DEPRESSION

In late 1929, the United States experienced the worst business collapse in its history. The Great Depression, as it came to be called, lasted well into the 1930s, almost until the beginning of World War II in Europe (1939-1945).

During the 1920s, banks loaned money for very little interest. The government even printed more money when there was a shortage of funds to lend. Because borrowing was so easy, many people borrowed money to buy stocks.

By 1929 banks were running short of funds. They began to ask people to repay their loans. Many people had to sell everything, including stocks, to come up with the money to repay the banks. With so much stock being sold at once, stock prices fell quickly, and the stock market "crashed," or closed down, on October 29, 1929. Many people lost their savings, nobody had money to buy anything extra, and many businesses shut down. Thirteen million people—nearly one-fourth of the U.S. labor force—were unemployed.

Presidents Herbert Hoover and Franklin Roosevelt, who succeeded Hoover, tried to get business running again. One way was by creating government projects to employ people. Although Hoover Dam was planned before the Great Depression, its funding came through right in the middle of the era. The dam became one of the government's employment projects.

During the Great Depression, temporary soup kitchens fed those who were unemployed and homeless.

Even though construction was months from starting, people everywhere knew that a big dam was going to be built near Las Vegas. Every day more and more people arrived, hoping to be hired. They arrived in wheezing automobiles, empty boxcars, on horseback, or on foot. Most of them had never seen a bulldozer in their life, let alone worked on a dam.

By the time Six Companies won the bid, Las Vegas was full of unemployed mechanics, store clerks, factory workers, lawyers, bankers, and students looking for work. The U.S. Labor Department had opened an office in downtown Las Vegas to help Six Companies with the hiring. By the time Crowe arrived, more than twenty-four hundred men had filed applications. The office had received more than twelve thousand letters inquiring about work.

But work on the dam was a long way off. The unemployed arrivals faced months of living in patched tents pitched on parched desert sand. Ragged encampments sprang up in and around town.

Close to the dam site, where the boat launch for Black Canyon was located, a squalid town of nearly one thousand residents developed. Sprawling from the rocky banks of the Colorado and out into the desert, the town consisted of tattered tents, cardboard houses, and rusty automobiles. The encampment soon became known as Ragtown.

One of the communities of canvas and cardboard in Black Canyon was called Ragtown.

As the local newspaper noted, "A 'pitiful and pathetic sight' is describing in the mildest possible language conditions that exist here in Las Vegas due to the influx of the hundreds that have come seeking work."

East Coast journalists who came to cover the story of the building of the dam were appalled by what they saw. The human situation was bad enough, but the setting was even worse. A reporter for the *New York Times Magazine* reported back, "Its sparse vegetation. . . rises out of it like blisters baked black. Furnace-like winds blowing. . . dust through the sheer sunlight of the desert give the sand hills, the jagged mountains a few miles off to the northeast, and to the very air a curious look of incandescence [glowing]."

The government's timetable allowed six months of preliminary work before construction started. This included erecting worker housing. Because of the bad economy and high unemployment, President Hoover asked that Six Companies start the work immediately—to get those unemployed men working and on the payroll.

Instead of building housing first and getting things in place, Crowe was going to have to do everything at the same time. The first workers on the project would have to

TENT CITIES

As the start date for Hoover Dam drew closer, several tent cities—full of would-be dam workers and their families—grew up around Black Canyon. McKeeversville and Ragtown were two of the largest.

Michael McKeever, a cook who worked for the government, had pitched his tent on the north slope of Hemenway Wash (a dry streambed), north of the dam site. As the site stirred to life, hundreds of people left Las Vegas and pitched their tents around McKeever's. Almost overnight, a tent city of several hundred families swelled out over Hemenway Wash. It was called McKeeversville in honor of its first resident. McKeeversville quickly became overcrowded, and other would-be workers started another tent town closer to the river.

At the foot of Hemenway Wash, Murl Emory ran a small store and boat service. He also worked as a guide for the Bureau of Reclamation expeditions on the river. Like McKeever's tent, Emory's store became the nucleus of a sprawling tent city. Originally it was called Williamsville, in honor of United States Marshall Claude Williams (who pitched his own tent among the squatters in an effort to provide law and order in the area). Its name quickly became Ragtown because of its ragged appearance.

provide their own housing. Most of them would be living in tents in workers' campgrounds, with no running water, electricity, or toilets. Even in March, temperatures were climbing toward 100 degrees Fahrenheit (38 degrees Celsius). In a few months, the temperature would be closer to 120 degrees Fahrenheit (49 degrees Celsius). It was going to be tough. The Six Companies contract required the company to provide housing for at least 80 percent of the dam workers. But it would be several months before worker housing would be available.

WHERE TO START?

The morning of March 13, 1931, a caravan of government vehicles pulled into Ragtown. Frank Crowe got out of the lead car, strode to the river, and got into a wooden boat. In less than ten minutes, he had floated downstream to the site. The return voyage upstream took nearly forty minutes, with the boat motor running at full speed. Even when the river appeared placid, the current of the Colorado was fierce.

That evening Crowe made a list of things that needed to be done immediately. The Union Pacific Railroad had already laid 23 miles (37 km) of track between Las Vegas and the site, so supplies could be delivered efficiently. The government had completed a gravel road between the site and Las Vegas. Still, it would be months before the government could supply Black Canyon with electrical power.

Crowe's first goal was to get the site opened up for work. The dam was being built in the canyon, not on the rim 1,200 feet (366 m) above. Men and equipment couldn't be lowered into the canyon on ropes for the entire time it took to build the project. And they couldn't work only from barges tethered to the walls. Shelves had to be blasted in the walls of the canyon so roads and rail systems could reach the bottom.

INTO THE CANYON

In just two weeks, nearly five hundred men were put on the Six Companies' payroll, and by April 1 the work was well under way. Crowe organized blasting and drilling crews and ran two shifts a day. Men were armed with pneumatic drills and boxes of dynamite. They were loaded onto boats at the Ragtown landing and floated into the site. From dawn until dark, the canyon hummed with activity and shook with the roar of dynamite explosions.

The canyon walls, rising straight out of the water, offered no toehold. At first the men did work from barges anchored to the canyon walls. Using drills powered by gasoline generators, they hammered out small ledges in the sheer rock face. Once there was a place to stand, they drilled holes in the rock, stuffed them with dynamite, and blasted out a bigger area. Because the initial work space was so small, all the debris had to be cleared by hand. When the road and rail beds were established, large equipment could get in to move it.

Workers who handled dynamite were called powder monkeys.

In this manner, 21 miles (34 km) of railroad lines were laid so supplies and heavy equipment could be brought down to river level. Several miles of excavated roadway also wove down the sheer face of the canyon so tractors, trucks, and other motorized vehicles could reach the river's edge.

The work was grueling and hazardous. Six Companies demanded that the crews work quickly. The first work in Black Canyon set the tone: speed was more important than safety. With so many people unemployed, if someone objected to the unsafe conditions or didn't want to do a specific job, he would be fired immediately. There was always someone else who would be happy to have the work.

Not surprisingly, accidents occurred regularly. With dynamite and rocks involved, many accidents were deadly. On May 8, a lit-

WHO ARE YOU DIGGING FOR?

After a dynamite blast in Tunnel No. 2, Floyd Huntington, the tunnel supervisor, entered the tunnel with worker Lee Ryan and a tractor operator. The three men were cautiously checking for loose rock when the tunnel ceiling suddenly gave way, filling the tunnel with rocks. Huntington and the tractor operator picked themselves up from the floor, but Ryan was nowhere to be seen. Huntington quickly sounded the alarm, and workers raced into the tunnel to dig for Ryan.

Meanwhile Ryan had raced from the tunnel when he realized the ceiling was falling. After swallowing a quick drink of water, he grabbed a shovel and ran back into the tunnel to help with the recovery. He soon found himself digging next to Huntington and asked, "Who's buried?"

The grim-faced superintendent put down his shovel, glared at Ryan, and bellowed, "You, you [jerk]."

tle more than one month after work started, a crew working at river level didn't hear the warning that a dynamite blast was about to go off 200 feet (61 m) overhead. One worker was blown 50 feet (15 m) through the air. He landed on a boulder and severely injured his back. Another worker was hit by a piece of flying rock that ripped off his ear and fractured his skull.

Only a few days later, a crew of four workers was standing on a ledge when it suddenly disintegrated. They tumbled into the canyon in an avalanche of rocks and dust. Hundreds of men witnessed the disaster and rushed to the site. With crowbars and shovels, they began digging frantically to try to find the men. Miraculously, two of the workers were discovered almost immediately. One escaped with only bruises. The other suffered a broken leg. Encouraged, everyone kept digging, hoping to find the other two alive. Eight hours later, the two men were found at the bottom of the rock pile, crushed beyond recognition.

During the height of construction, first-aid stations in the canyon treated more than fifteen hundred people each month. Speed and the accidents it caused prompted a phrase that circulated among the workers: "Build a dam, kill a man."

In mid-May, although the rail beds and roads still weren't finished, the second phase of construction started. By this time, there were eleven hundred men on the Six Companies' payroll. Frank Crowe was ready to tackle the hardest part of the job—moving the Colorado River.

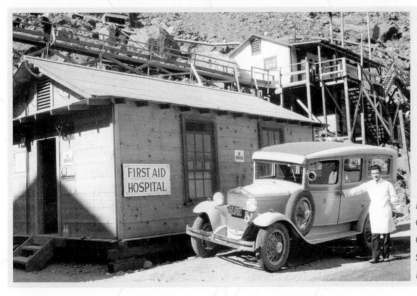

Far left, dynamite blasts and falling rocks kept first-aid stations at the dam site, such as this one, *near left,* busy.

Chapter Four
MOVING THE COLORADO RIVER
(1931–1932)

ON MAY 16, 1931, A HUGE dynamite explosion ripped a giant hole in the rock in Black Canyon. Construction had started on the diversion tunnels.

Six Companies had always thought the diversion tunnels would be the toughest part of the project. Although building a concrete dam sixty stories high would be difficult, they knew how to build dams and work with concrete. But before any dam could be built, the Colorado River had to be moved out of its bed.

It was impossible to move the Colorado out of the canyon. The

This broad view of early work at the dam site shows openings for the four river diversion tunnels. There are two on each side of the river.

canyon walls were too high. So the plan was to keep the river in Black Canyon and divert it around the dam site by blasting four tunnels through the rock, just above water level. Once the tunnels were done, a temporary cofferdam would be erected. This would force the river into the tunnels.

The bottom of the canyon would be dry for the length of the tunnels, a distance of a little less than 1 mile (1.6 km). This would allow workers to excavate the riverbed and erect the dam. When the dam was completed, the tunnels would be closed, the cofferdam blasted away, and the river would again flow through the bottom of the canyon. Only then would it encounter Hoover Dam.

On paper, the plans for the diversion tunnels were detailed, concise, and sensible. The Bureau of Reclamation and Six Companies had spent thousands of hours working it all out. Finally it was time to actually put the plans to work under the searing sun of the Nevada desert.

TIMING THE TUNNELS

Six Companies' contract demanded that the Colorado River be diverted by October 1, 1933. Even so, the speed with which Frank Crowe was opening up the canyon and starting on the tunnels amazed Bureau of Reclamation officials. Elwood Mead, bureau commissioner, commented to the press, "Those western dirt-moving fools are building highways, starting tunnels, and laying railroads all at once, but without any mix-ups."

> "Those western dirt-moving fools are building highways, starting tunnels, and laying railroads all at once, but without any mix-ups."
>
> —**Elwood Meade**

Crowe had two reasons to work so fast. First, Six Companies would be fined three thousand dollars for each day of work beyond the October 1, 1933, deadline.

Second, the Colorado River could only be diverted between November and February, when its water level was low. Once the spring thaws started in the mountains, the river would swell to a raging torrent. From March through October, the river was capable of breaking through any cofferdam in its path. Crowe had to divert the river during the fall and winter of 1932, because he wouldn't have another chance until after the deadline.

Failure to divert the river in the time specified could cost Six Companies hundreds of thousands of dollars. It would also eat up the firm's profits, including Frank Crowe's percentage of them.

STARTING THE TUNNELS

Three entries were started simultaneously for each diversion tunnel. The work included an entry portal upstream where the water would come in; the exit portal, nearly a mile downstream; and an adit, or cross, tunnel opening in the middle.

Excavating adit tunnels was extra work, but they allowed the main tunneling to progress at a faster pace. Two crews entered the adit and traveled to where it met the middle of the main tunnel. Then they worked backward toward each opening. That way four crews could excavate each tunnel at the same time. Altogether more than twelve hundred men could be kept working on tunnel excavation.

The adit tunnel on the Arizona side of the river was started first. Because the roads into the canyon weren't completed, the crews floated into the canyon on huge barges loaded with gasoline-powered generators, diesel-powered air compressors, jackhammers, drills, and even a portable blacksmith shop complete with a furnace and drill sharpener.

A blaze of white paint left by the survey crews marked the spot on the canyon wall where the tunnel would open. The barges were anchored to the wall with iron rings and tethered into place. The men leaped onto a tiny gravel beach, not even big enough for a small tractor, and began to jackhammer the rock, shoveling the debris by hand and loading it onto the barges.

The adit tunnel on the Nevada side of the river was an even tougher project. There wasn't even a small gravel beach, so the men had to

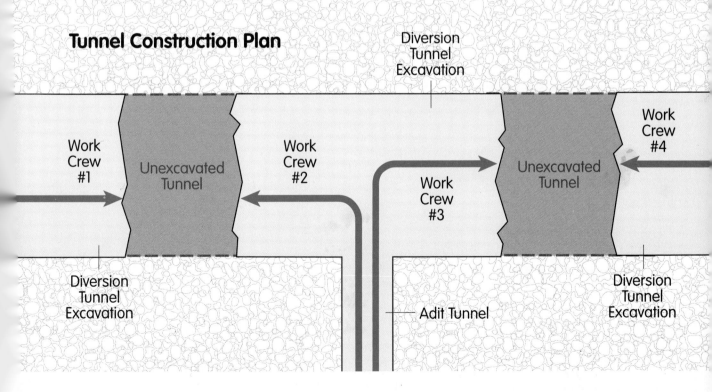

Tunnel Construction Plan

Diversion Tunnel Excavation

Work Crew #1

Unexcavated Tunnel

Work Crew #2

Work Crew #3

Unexcavated Tunnel

Work Crew #4

Diversion Tunnel Excavation

Adit Tunnel

Diversion Tunnel Excavation

drive ringbolts into the canyon wall and string a cable suspension footbridge between them. Then they jackhammered the rock to create a small ledge to stand on.

Once the workers gained a foothold, they used dynamite to speed the opening of the tunnels. Other work crews built a trestle bridge across the Colorado so that trucks could travel between the two sides.

EXCAVATING THE DIVERSION TUNNELS

The diversion tunnels would be 56 feet (17 m) in diameter and 4,000 feet (1,220 m) long. This made each one as wide as a four-lane highway, as tall as a five-story office building, and more than three-quarters of a mile (1.2 km) long. Since they were too huge to blast all at once, Frank Crowe devised a plan that broke each tunnel into five zones for excavation.

A 12-by-12 foot (3.6-by-3.6 m) heading in the middle of the top of the tunnel was excavated first. From there, the workers could stand upright and excavate the wedge-shaped side sections of the top, called wings. When these three sections were done (the heading in the middle, with a wing on either side), the upper 12 feet (4 m) of the tunnel, complete with curving sides, was open.

The next section, the bench, formed the middle portion of the tunnel. Measuring 56 feet (17 m) wide and 30 feet (9 m) tall, the bench was the toughest part of the excavation because it was so large. Once this section was excavated, the tunnel was 42 feet (13 m) high. The sides and top of the tunnel formed the curves of a circle, but the bottom was still flat.

The last excavation section at the bottom of the tunnel, the invert, brought the tunnel up to its full 56 feet (17 m) diameter and gave it a circular shape. For this section, 14 feet (4 m) of rock was excavated from the bottom, and the sides of the invert were then curved to meet with the walls of the bench section.

THE WILLIAMS JUMBO

The excavations of the headings and wing sections weren't too difficult because the sections were only 12 feet (3.6 m) high. The miners could drill and blast in a normal fashion. They jackhammered holes into the rock, filled the holes with dynamite, blasted, and then cleared away the rubble, or muck, as it was called. But if Six Companies was

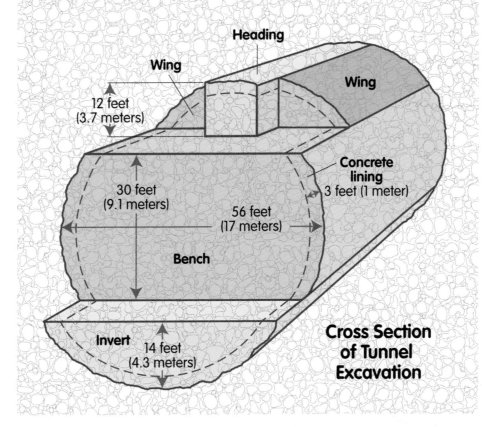

Heading

Wing

12 feet
(3.7 meters)

Wing

**Concrete
lining**
3 feet (1 meter)

30 feet
(9.1 meters)

56 feet
(17 meters)

Bench

**Cross Section
of Tunnel
Excavation**

Invert   14 feet
(4.3 meters)

going to make its deadline for diverting the Colorado River, some other technique had to be devised to excavate the giant bench sections much faster.

The tunnel drilling crews were large, usually thirty men, because the more holes drilled at one time, the faster the excavation. The problem with excavating the bench section was how to get thirty men 30 feet (9 m) up in the air without ladders or scaffolding. Six Companies needed to drill, blast, and muck quickly. They couldn't spend time putting up and taking down ladders and scaffolding. Frank Crowe turned the problem over to his assistant superintendent, Bernard "Woody" Williams.

Previous dam-building projects had used mules and horses, but Woody Williams knew machines were needed for this excavation. Williams mounted four wooden platforms onto the bed of a huge truck built especially for the army during World War I (1914–1918). The miners and the chuck tenders (workers who helped maintain the drills) stood on two of the platforms. The other two platforms held the racks of drills. Fully loaded with men and their drills, the truck looked like a giant, bristling porcupine.

The men called the truck the Williams Jumbo. They backed it into the tunnel, right up to one side of the rock face. It took about twenty minutes to hook up the power lines. Then the workers began drilling. When they finished, they would move the jumbo to the other half of the tunnel face. Then the miners drilled out the other side of the tunnel. They filled the drill holes on both sides with dynamite. Then they disconnected everything and drove the jumbo out of the tunnel so the dynamite could be detonated. When the tunnel was safe, the muck trucks moved in and cleared away the debris. The whole process took about four hours.

SCALERS' DANGEROUS AND DARING WORK

Directly after a blast, before the muck was cleared, the tunnel had to be checked for loose rocks in the

Above, Woody Williams designed a movable three-story drilling platform *(right).* It greatly sped up excavation of the diversion tunnels. The rig came to be known as the Williams Jumbo.

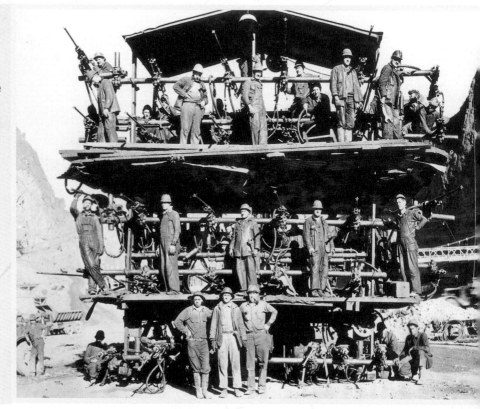

tunnel walls. The first person in was the safety miner. Because of Six Companies' deadline, safety miners usually entered the tunnel before the dust had even settled.

Safety miners knew mining so well, the other workers joked, they could smell a loose rock. If the safety miner gave the "all clear" sign, the electric shovel and tractors moved in to load the muck onto trucks. If anything seemed loose, the safety miners called in the scalers.

Scalers were men chosen for their ability to think quickly and move fast. The scalers, on ladders, working with crowbars, were responsible for getting any loose rocks off the tunnel walls. At the Hoover Dam site, the workers said that there were only two kinds of scalers: quick ones and dead ones. Because scalers only worked in situations where the rock was unstable, their job was always hazardous.

The most spectacular and dangerous job of all belonged to the high scalers. These workers cleared loose rocks from the canyon walls. While scalers worked primarily in the tunnels, the high scalers dangled on ropes, hundreds of feet above the canyon floor.

Frank Crowe didn't want loose rocks dropping from the

These high scalers are working 550 feet (168 m) above the river at the site for the Arizona intake towers.

These two Apache men worked as high scalers. Native Americans from the Yaqui, Crow, and Navajo nations also worked as high scalers at the dam site.

canyon walls into the site. Even a small pebble falling from a height of 1,000 feet (305 m) would split a man's skull like a meat cleaver. Crowe also needed a smooth wall surface on which to anchor the concrete sides of the dam. Centuries of wind, rain, and blowing dust had left the walls of Black Canyon fractured and pockmarked. Even the tiniest flakes of loose rock had to be removed.

High scalers had to be agile and strong, with no fear of heights. Sitting on wooden planks and loaded with water bags, crowbars, and wrenches, the high scalers were lowered over the rim into the canyon. They dangled there against the canyon wall. Once the scalers were in place, the 44-pound (20-kilogram) jackhammers and bundles of steel drill bits were lowered over the edge to them.

High scalers spent the next eight hours gripping a roaring jackhammer, hammering away at loose pieces of rock. A frayed rope, a momentary lapse of attention, a second of dizziness from the heat, or failure to hear a warning from above could mean instant death. The canyon wall was a tangle of power lines and hoses to power the drills. High scalers had to be careful not to hit any of these lines, or they might be electrocuted. When their shift was done, they crawled up the ropes, hand-over-hand, back up to the rim. They carried their equipment, which weighed about as much as two bicycles, on their backs.

As work on Hoover Dam progressed, the site became a tourist attraction. The high scalers were the main event. Several high scalers became known for their daring exploits, sometimes pushing off the wall and swinging out 100 feet (30 m) into the canyon for the benefit of sightseers.

The most spectacular high-scaling feat was performed by Oliver Cowan and Arnold Parks. One afternoon Burl Rutledge, a Bureau of Reclamation engineer, was on the rim of the canyon to examine a portion of the cliff. He leaned out too far and slipped. As he began tumbling into the canyon, Cowan and Parks heard the sound of his fall above them. Cowan pushed off from the wall, swung over, and intercepted Rutledge by catching his leg as he fell. Parks, arriving a second later, grabbed Rutledge's upper body and pinned it to the canyon wall. The two men held the stunned engineer in place until a line was rigged from above and he could be hauled to safety.

SPEED AND DEADLY TUNNELS

On June 25, 1931, the electrical transmission lines into the site were completed. With the flick of a switch, Frank Crowe had 80,000 volts of power to work with. Not having to rely on gasoline-powered generators moved everything along faster. The tunnels could be adequately lighted, and more drills could be added. Most importantly for Six Companies, this meant that they could work on the dam twenty-four hours a day. A third eight-hour work shift was added.

Even though families had little money for travel during the Great Depression, high scalers drew many groups of tourists (above) to the construction zone.

In direct violation of the Nevada mining laws, Six Companies used regular gasoline- and diesel-powered vehicles, even in the tunnels. The company should have been using exhaust-free, electrically powered vehicles in the tunnels, or an electric rail system. Gas-powered vehicles release carbon monoxide exhaust, a deadly poison. As work progressed, carbon monoxide accumulated in the tunnels and caused severe health problems for the workers and sometimes even death.

On November 7, 1931, when work in the tunnels had been going on for roughly six months, Nevada's state inspector of mines ordered Six Companies to stop using gasoline-powered trucks to haul muck out of the tunnels. Six Companies' response was to file a lawsuit against the state of Nevada. The lawsuit claimed that tunneling wasn't really mining, and the state of Nevada should leave the company alone. Six Companies also claimed that it couldn't afford to convert the vehicles to electricity.

> "Our directors would rather take a loss of $100,000 than to hurt one man."
>
> —Frank Crowe

Six Companies continued to use gasoline-powered trucks while the case was in the courts. Workers continued to get sick and die. The case dragged on for so long— because of the stalling tactics of the Six Companies lawyers—that the tunnels were finished by the time it came before a judge. While the judge indicated that he agreed with the mining inspector, he also thought the whole complaint was pointless since the tunnels were virtually finished. Ultimately, the courts ruled in favor of Six Companies. Getting Hoover Dam built was a top

Continued use of gasoline-powered construction vehicles in the tunnels contradicted Frank Crowe's claim that Six Companies was concerned about workers' health.

priority, even in the courts. The courts and Six Companies considered the tunnel "problem" finished.

During a Thanksgiving Day speech to the workers that year, Frank Crowe said, "Our directors would rather take a loss of $100,000 than to hurt one man." The workers couldn't help but notice, however, how frequently people became sick in the tunnels. Four years later, the problem would return to haunt Six Companies.

THE COLORADO STRIKES

Work on the tunnels progressed speedily throughout the summer of 1931. Even the river seemed to be cooperating. Its level remained constant, and the current flowed smoothly. Then in September, a series of thunderstorms struck in the mountains east of Black Canyon. Roaring down through gullies and streams, the rainwater thundered into the Colorado River. Without warning, on the night of September 26, a flash flood reached the dam site.

LABOR STRIKES

Most of the men employed at Hoover Dam needed the work, but they did not like the working conditions. The dam was built just as the idea of organizing workers to strike against unfair employers was growing in the United States. One of the first strikes in the country occurred at the dam in August 1931.

In early August, when Six Companies announced that it was cutting wages for a few tunnel workers, twelve hundred dam workers walked off the job, *below*. They were already disgruntled by the heat, lack of safety standards at the site, and poor living conditions.

Six Companies quickly fired the striking workers and hired new workers from the pool of unemployed men in Las Vegas. Some of the "new" hires were actually the skilled "old" workers who had been fired for striking.

Other labor problems arose at Hoover Dam, as well as another strike in 1935. During these disputes, management never gave in to labor's demands. If the workers didn't like the conditions at the dam, they could leave. Six Companies could always replace them.

Three floods in 1932 destroyed equipment and delayed work on the dam.

Men working in the tunnels that night heard the quickening gurgle of the river and a faint breathy rushing. Then the floodwater was climbing up the walls of the canyon with terrifying speed. In only a few hours, the river rose 12 feet (3.6 m), lapping at the opening of the Arizona adit tunnel.

The water subsided as quickly as it came. The shaken workers told themselves that it was September, the start of the low water season. There would be no more floods until spring. They were wrong.

During the first week of a warm February 1932, rain, instead of snow, fell in the mountains northeast of Black Canyon. That month three separate floods hit the site. During the first two floods, the machine shops flooded, and the trestle bridge across Black Canyon was swallowed up. Sandbag dikes (barriers) had to be built at the entrance of the upstream tunnel portals to prevent flooding there. The third flood melted the sandbag dikes like sugar. The Colorado rose 17 feet (5 m) in the tunnels in three hours.

It took all the workers more than a week to clean up the mess left by the third flood. Trying to get the mud out of the tunnels was almost impossible. It was too thick to pump (it clogged every pump) and too thin to shovel (like trying to pick up creamy soup with a fork). In the end, the workers removed as much as they could and left the rest to harden on the floor of the tunnels and to be jackhammered out with the remaining invert sections.

CONCRETE IN THE TUNNELS

On March 16, 1932, excavation on Tunnel No. 3 on the Arizona side of the river was finished, and concrete pouring started. The government specifications called for all four tunnels to be lined with 3 feet (1 m) of concrete. This would reduce each tunnel's diameter from 56 to 50 feet (17 to 15 m). The concrete's smooth surface would allow the river to flow more easily than through rough rock walls.

To pour the concrete, curved wooden molds were constructed 3 feet (1 m) out from the tunnel walls.

Workmen spread concrete in Tunnel No. 4.

The concrete was pumped into the space between the tunnel wall and the mold. Once the concrete hardened, the mold was pulled away and a smooth surface remained.

The pace of work to finish Tunnels No. 3 and No. 4, the two Arizona tunnels, was relentless. They had to be ready by low-water season so that the river could be diverted through them. Tunnels No. 1 and No. 2, on the Nevada side, would be finished shortly after. They would be ready to divert the rest of the river during the high-water season.

The crews worked hard, but Frank Crowe worked even harder. It seemed as though he never slept, as if he were everywhere. At 3:00 A.M., during one graveyard shift, two workers were discussing how to pour the concrete. Seemingly out of nowhere, echoing through the tunnel, a voice barked out, "Who is holding up this pour?" The two turned around to see Frank Crowe stalking off.

Above, to pour concrete over workers' heads, laborers dumped buckets of cement into hoppers on top of this rig. Two 8-inch (20-centimeter) steel and rubber pipes, one on each side of a second rig (not shown), forced the concrete into the molds overhead by means of pressurized air.
Right, at last, the first river water exits Diversion Tunnel No. 3.

DIVERTING THE RIVER

On November 13, 1932—eleven months ahead of schedule—Tunnels No. 3 and No. 4 were finished. Six Companies was ready to divert the Colorado River. That morning one hundred dump trucks loaded with broken rock lined the road leading to the trestle bridge that spanned the river. The thick muddy water swirled smoothly below the planks.

By 11:30 A.M., everything was ready. Frank Crowe gave the signal to start dumping. Every fifteen seconds, a truck began dumping debris. This pace continued into the next shift. The water level rose higher and higher, as the river strained to keep above the underwater rocky barrier that was developing.

The dumping continued through the night. At 7:30 the next morning, the top of the diversion dam broke the surface of the water. The muddy water spun and whirled as it tried—and failed—to climb over the barrier. Then the water began backing up and heading toward the mouth of Tunnel No. 4. For a few seconds, the water lingered on the lip of the tunnel. Then, with a surge, it rushed in, pushing an enormous wave of foam ahead of itself.

> "She's taking it, boys. By God, she's taking it!"
>
> **—a worker at Tunnel No. 4**

A cheer rose up from the people gathered on the banks when the workman stationed at the entrance began waving his hat and yelled, "She's taking it, boys. By God, she's taking it!" The Colorado River had left its bed in Black Canyon.

Chapter Five
MODEL CITY AND MORE
(1931–1932)

BY SEPTEMBER 1931, EVERY PART of the Hoover Dam project was well under way. The site excavation and the four diversion tunnels were completed. A gravel-processing plant, two concrete mixing facilities, and a city for the workers and their families were under construction.

The government had decided to include a city at an early stage in the plans. Workers at previous dams had found their own housing, usually living in tents at the site. But Hoover Dam was different.

It was obvious to the first survey crews that no dam would get built in the area, especially on the government's timetable, unless decent housing was provided for the workers. No dam had ever been built in such an extreme climate. With an estimated five thousand workers on the project, the crew was just too big to house in tents.

Above, living in tents in the extreme climate of the Nevada desert posed many health hazards. *Right,* workers' children made the best of camp life until houses could be built for their families in Boulder City.

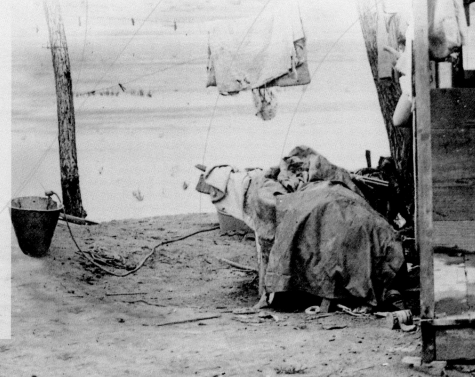

In addition, Hoover Dam was going to be a demonstration to the world. Three presidents were involved: Coolidge initiated it, Hoover started it, and Roosevelt finished it. All three of them viewed the dam as a showcase for American technology. Nothing, especially the location, must be allowed to sabotage the project. Decent housing for workers was just another part of the technological demonstration.

BUILDING A TOWN FROM SCRATCH

When survey crews first looked at the region, the town of Las Vegas seemed the logical place for worker housing. But early on, Las Vegas was rejected because it was too wild. Drinking and gambling were the mainstays of the town's economy. Las Vegas was no place to house five thousand dam workers with a serious job to do. In order for the workers to stay focused on the job, they needed separate housing, away from Las Vegas. Given the number of workers, their housing would become an entire city.

A site in the desert 7 miles (11 km) from the dam was chosen. The soon-to-be town was given the named Boulder City. Until then no one had built a complete town from scratch.

The federal government had hired S. R. DeBoer, an award-winning Denver, Colorado, architect, to draw up the initial plans for the city. Since the whole point of Hoover Dam was to provide water and power to the western region, DeBoer saw no reason not to take advantage of those potential resources. His plans called for a complex with lush public spaces, tree-lined avenues, even a golf course. Curving streets would pass buildings with green lawns and flower beds.

Six Companies looked at DeBoer's architectural plans and threw them out. It would cost too much to lay out circular streets. Crowe put the town on a square grid with straight streets, took out most of the green spaces, and started building.

A machine shop, a temporary mess hall, temporary bunkhouses, and a rail yard were the first to be completed. Back in March, Six Companies had built a rough bunkhouse right in the canyon, close to the water's edge. While it was better than the tents at Ragtown, it wasn't much better. Crowe wanted his unmarried workers out of the canyon bunkhouse and into

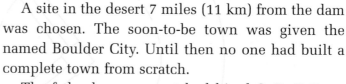

Below top, rough bunkhouses were built in Black Canyon to house workers until housing was ready in Boulder City, *below bottom.*

decent housing, so dormitories had top priority. By June the first of eight permanent bunkhouses was completed, and workers began moving in.

As soon as the Boulder City dormitories were done, one-, two-, and three-bedroom cottages were built for the married workers and their families. A commercial district for stores, a hospital, and a recreation center completed the town. By November 1931, nearly all the workers were out of Ragtown and living in Boulder City.

LIVING IN BOULDER CITY

Boulder City was built for the workers, but it wasn't free to them. The daily charge for a cubicle in the dormitory and three meals was $1.65. One-, two-, and three-bedroom cottages for married men rented for $15, $19, and $30 a month, respectively.

The average laborer earned $4 a day, so most men ended up spending more than 40 percent of their paycheck on food and housing. This was a stiff price. But after the hardships most had experienced during the Great Depression, most workers considered themselves lucky to have a job and a place to live. They were happy to pay the stiff price.

Although Boulder City was built in Nevada, it was not subject to the laws of Nevada. There was no elected mayor or other town officials. The city was controlled by a city manager appointed by the federal government. In keeping with the federal government's distrust and dislike of Las Vegas, no alcohol or gambling was permitted.

For most of the period of construction of Hoover Dam, the streets of Boulder City were bare of vegetation. Wind whistled down the streets, blowing sand into every crevice. The dormitories and cottages were stark, but compared to tents pitched on broiling desert sand, they were luxurious. One worker who moved into a tiny cottage with his wife and daughter said what most of them felt, "To us, it was beautiful."

In December 1931, the Bureau of Reclamation sent one of its landscape gardeners to Boulder City to "green" the city. Wilbur Weed ordered and planted more than nine thousand trees. Most of the trees were still quite small when construction was finished on the dam.

The mess hall served meals around the clock. It was the social center of Boulder City, and it was the site of the first dance, attended by more than two thousand men and women, on Thanksgiving eve, 1931.

Bureau of Reclamation landscape gardener Wilbur Weed *(holding the tree)* supervised workers on landscaping projects in Boulder City. They planted more than nine thousand trees.

SIX THOUSAND MEALS DAILY

The effort involved in feeding thousands of workers three meals a day was almost as relentless as the work on the dam. Because dam construction went on twenty-four hours a day, the dining room had to supply meals to three different shifts.

The Boulder City mess hall, *above,* could seat 1,150 men at a time, eight men to a table. All workers were allowed to eat as much of anything as they wanted at any meal. Box lunches were prepared to take to the work site. A staff of thirty white-clad waiters served more than six thousand meals every day.

Six Companies paid a supply company, Anderson Brothers, to handle all the food purchasing and preparation. The quantities of food shipped in each week were staggering: 13 tons (11.8 metric tons) of fruits and vegetables, 5 tons (4.5 metric tons) of meat, 2 tons (1.8 metric tons) of potatoes, 2.5 tons (2.3 metric tons) of eggs, and 1.5 tons (1.4 metric tons) of other groceries.

The demand for milk, butter, and cheese was so great that Anderson Brothers purchased a 160-acre (65-hectare) ranch about 80 miles (129 km) from Black Canyon. Anderson built its own dairy there and stocked the ranch with one hundred dairy cows. Day and night, caravans of ice-cooled trucks carried the milk and other dairy products into Boulder City.

The dance was such a success that Saturday night dances became a regular feature of Boulder City social life. Christmas pageants, political rallies, and other meetings were also held in the mess hall.

Hoover Dam was a national story. Journalists were at the site every day. Most of these journalists also visited the model city that was rising in the desert, only 7 miles (11 km) from the dam, and wrote many articles about it. Boulder City was a national story in its own right.

GRAVEL, GRAVEL, AND MORE GRAVEL

Hoover Dam was never a sedate, orderly project that progressed one step at a time. Canyon walls were jackhammered, tunnels were blasted, dormitories were built, and rail lines were laid—all at the same time. While Boulder City was being constructed and the diversion tunnels were being blasted, a huge gravel-processing plant was being constructed 2 miles (3 km) west of the river.

Gravel is a key ingredient of concrete. Concrete is made by mixing aggregate (sand and crushed rock, usually gravel) with Portland cement and water. Aggregate was the most important part of the mix.

TWENTY-FOUR AFRICAN AMERICAN WORKERS

None of the first one thousand men hired to work on Hoover Dam was African American. Six Companies claimed to be afraid of racial unrest.

Only twenty-four African Americans worked on the dam, and they were assigned to the gravel pits, the hottest place in the whole Hoover Dam project. They weren't allowed to live in Boulder City either. They had to commute 30 miles (48 km) from West Las Vegas in segregated buses. These workers were even forced to drink from separate water buckets at the site.

It would make up approximately three-fourths of the dam's mass.

Bureau of Reclamation engineers had combed the area, searching for high-quality gravel. They chose a natural gravel deposit about 6 miles (10 km) upstream from the site. The gravel there covered more than 100 acres (40 hectares) and was 30 feet (9 m) deep in most places.

The gravel-processing plant constructed for Hoover Dam was enormous. The huge steel-sided building, surrounded by piles of gravel, sat in the middle of the desert. Conveyor belts carried an endless stream of rock. Only a few control panel operators were needed to run it.

The gravel-processing plant was a vital part of the dam project. Yet in the end, the $450,000 plant left no trace. When Hoover Dam was finished, the entire plant disappeared under the waters of the newly formed reservoir.

Six Companies' gravel-processing plant supplied gravel for the concrete used to build Hoover Dam.

WORKER TRANSPORT

Six Companies was a stickler for starting each shift on time. So it provided the transportation. About a half-hour before the start of each shift, the workers would assemble at the mess hall and rumble off to work in enormous buses, *left.*

Each held 154 men. Eight hours later, they boarded the buses at the site to go back to the mess hall in Boulder City.

The company also devised special transport systems to get the men in and out of the canyon. The workers were loaded onto small skips or cable cars, *below right,* at the rim of the canyon and were lowered over the edge, directed by hand signals from an operator onboard the skip. Workers were also lowered into the canyon on monkey slides, or platforms that moved up and down the canyon walls on greased poles or skids.

A ride on either of these could be a harrowing experience. Sometimes the ropes for a skip became twisted. This caused it to spin wildly as it was lowered into the canyon. A confusion over hand signals could send the skip crashing into the canyon wall. On New Year's Day in 1933, forty-five workers crashed into the Arizona side of the canyon. Many workers were hospitalized. Five uninjured workers were so terrified by the experience that they quit their jobs on the spot.

This was one of the trains that hauled gravel to the Six Companies gravel-processng plant.

GRAVEL CARS AND RAIL ACCIDENTS

Railroad lines connected the plant to the dam site. Trains chugged back and forth, delivering the crushed aggregate to the concrete mixing facilities and immediately returning for another load. With railcars fully loaded with rocks, the potential for an accident was always present.

One afternoon in January 1932, a crew was inspecting the railroad trestle that spanned the Colorado River and linked the gravel operations to the dam site. Just as they were finishing up, a call came through on the portable phone that linked them to the gravel-processing plant. A runaway train was coming down the tracks, heading straight for the work crew.

The crew scrambled into action. A pile driver (a piece of machinery used to construct rail lines) was sitting on the tracks. If the runaway train plowed into it, the crash would send everything careening into the trestle and most probably destroy it.

The men put their shoulders to the pile driver and pushed as hard as they could. It wouldn't budge. Desperate, the crew spied an empty railcar sitting on a level section of the tracks leading to the gravel-processing plant. They frantically swarmed over the car and bolted it to the tracks with steel cables and pins. In less than ten minutes, the car was securely tied to the tracks, where it would absorb the initial impact of a crash and prevent the destruction of the trestle.

The men then dropped everything and ran. Once away from the site, they stopped and waited, looking back anxiously at the tracks. Five minutes passed, then ten. Still nothing came down the tracks. Puzzled, the crew regrouped around the bolted railcar.

Finally a small locomotive came into view, chugging along slowly. It was clearly under the control of an engineer. It pulled up to the bolted railcar and stopped. Several men from the gravel-processing plant got out and walked around the car, amazed at the web of steel cables and spikes that bolted it to the tracks. Then they started to laugh.

Irritated, the crew leader demanded to know where the runaway train was. "Right there," said the plant supervisor with a smirk, "and from the looks of it, that's one [railcar] that won't ever run away again!"

MOUNTAINS OF CONCRETE

The government plans called for 4.4 million cubic yards (3.4 million cubic meters) of concrete to be poured. The government provided the basic materials for the concrete, but Six Companies had to furnish all the machinery, tools, and supplies. The dry air of the Nevada desert, as well as the structure of the dam itself, posed two problems for Frank Crowe. The concrete needed to have a lot of water mixed into it to keep it moist and pliable. Otherwise the dry desert climate would harden it by the time it was delivered to any location. Yet to line the diversion tunnels and build the dam, the concrete needed to be stiff, not soupy. If it were too soupy, it would ooze out of the forms and take too long to harden.

To solve the problem, Six Companies constructed two concrete mixing plants. One was called the "High Mix" and the other the "Low Mix." Both plants were located as close to the site as possible. That way, the cement could be mixed very dry, yet still reach the site in time.

Low Mix went into production on March 8, 1932. It ran almost continuously for the next three years. During that time, it produced almost 400,000 cubic yards (306,000 m³) of concrete, most of which went into lining the diversion tunnels.

This was enough concrete to build any dam that had been constructed before the Hoover Dam project. But at the Hoover Dam, most of that concrete was used to line the tunnels and for other parts of the project. High Mix went into production shortly after Low Mix, and most of its production went into construction of the dam itself.

At the High Mix concrete-mixing plant, trains dumped cement into the two silos from above. Gravel arrived by conveyor belt, *middle left,* and trucks, *bottom,* waited to haul freshly mixed concrete to construction sites at the dam.

SECURING THE DAM SITE

Building the cofferdams was the last project to be completed before work on the actual dam itself. Just dumping rocks into the river and forcing the Colorado to move into diversion tunnels wasn't enough. As soon as the river was diverted, crews scurried into the canyon and built two enormous earth-and-rock cofferdams.

The first cofferdam, constructed 500 feet (152 m) downstream from the diversion tunnels, was the largest because it had to be able to hold back the Colorado River during its high-water season. During the spring and

Water bubbling up in the foreground shows that the cofferdam under construction is about to break the surface of the water.

summer months, the Colorado raged with more than 150,000 cubic feet (4,200 m³) of water per second. The February 1932 flood that inundated the tunnels and halted work had only been 57,000 cubic feet (1,600 m³) per second, only about one-third of what the Colorado could hurl at them.

During November 1932, more than four thousand truckloads of fill were put into the upper cofferdam. When the structure was completed, it looked like a low, wide pyramid with a flat top. Later a smaller cofferdam was built 500 feet (152 m) downstream. It was just upstream from the exits of the diversion tunnels, to prevent the river water from backing up into the dam site.

Meanwhile, the high scalers were finishing their work. Hoover Dam needed to join a smooth surface, so the places where the canyon walls touched the dam were chiseled and tapered into a smooth "V" shape. Once that was done, the high scalers scored huge notches into the canyon walls, where the concrete of the dam would anchor into the canyon.

With the upstream cofferdam in place and the river flowing into the diversion tunnels, workers began excavating the river bottom. The dam had to sit on solid bedrock, so all the silt in the bottom of the riverbed had to be removed. Every day trucks hauled 22,000 cubic yards (17,000 m³) of silt and rock out of the canyon and dumped it into waiting railcars. Trains took the silt and rock upstream and unloaded it into small side canyons.

The three shifts competed with each other to see who could excavate and haul the most dirt. On January 24, 1933, the overnight swing-shift crew won. They disposed of 1,841 truckloads of dirt during their eight-hour shift—roughly one truckload of dirt every fifteen seconds.

On May 31, 1933, the last load of debris from the river bottom was hauled away. Workers had excavated 40 feet (12 m) of riverbed before finally hitting bedrock. Several springs that seeped through cracks in the rocks were filled in and sealed with grout, a thin cement mix, so seeping water wouldn't eat away at the foundation of the dam. Crews also installed a network of drainage pipes to funnel the water away from the dam site.

High scalers worked hard to smooth canyon walls.

While workers cleared the riverbed, carpenters were hard at work constructing large wooden boxes, the forms to hold the concrete for Hoover Dam. On June 6, 1933, Frank Crowe nodded his approval and the first bucket of concrete was poured. After twenty-six months of excavation and tunneling—along with building a city, two concrete-mixing plants, and a gravel-processing plant—Hoover Dam was going up.

GOLD?

The final excavation work was relentless drudgery, punctuated by small bits of excitement. A rumor circulated that gold nuggets had been found in the bottom of the canyon, causing a lot of excitement. There was never any gold in Black Canyon. The fact that it was April Fools' Day probably had something to do with the rumor.

Chapter Six
THE DAM GOES UP
(1933–1934)

AS IT ROSE FROM THE FLOOR of Black Canyon, Hoover Dam looked like a tumble of children's building blocks. Large wooden box forms, between 25 and 60 feet square (21 and 330 m²), were placed next to each other. The concrete was poured into these molds. It took 230 of these boxes to form the base of the dam.

Above, dam laborers install water pipes in a mold for concrete. Cold water running through the pipes helped the concrete harden faster.
Right, the boxes built to shape the concrete for the dam looked like children's building blocks.

PIPES, WATER, AND GROUT

Six Companies liked to work fast, but this part of the project would take more time. As concrete hardens, it creates a chemical reaction that produces heat. If Hoover Dam had been poured in one continuous block, its temperature would have risen 40 degrees Fahrenheit (4 degrees Celsius). It would have taken 125 years for the concrete to cool and harden, and it would have cracked in the process, making the dam useless. Even pouring concrete in 5-foot (1.5-m) layers created a lot of heat.

To meet their deadlines, Frank Crowe created an ingenious method for cooling the concrete. A network of thermometers and 1-inch (2.5-cm) pipes were laid in the wet concrete. Refrigerated water was run through the pipes to cool down and harden the concrete faster. The thermometers indicated when the concrete was cool enough to pour another layer. When the dam was finished, the pipes were pumped full of grout, which sealed them and strengthened the dam. By the time Hoover Dam reached its full height, 582 miles (937 km) of pipe had been laid.

To ensure the structure wouldn't be weakened by the tiny hairline cracks that remained between the concrete boxes, grout was pumped into these spaces once the molds were removed. To make doubly sure the grout bonded securely, the upstream and downstream sides of each mold were scored (scratched) with vertical grooves. The two other sides were scored with horizontal grooves. The grout bonded better to this rough surface, and the columns locked together in a solid unit.

HURRY UP AND THE GREAT DELAYER

As far as Frank Crowe was concerned, waiting for the concrete to harden was the hardest part of the job. So far, nearly everything had been left up to Six Companies. Crowe could go as fast or as slowly as he wanted, as long as he met their deadlines. But the Bureau of Reclamation controlled the speed of pouring the concrete for the dam structure.

The Bureau of Reclamation sent Walker Young to the dam site to make sure cement had enough time to dry properly as the dam went up.

The Six Companies contract stated that concrete could be poured no more than 5 feet (1.5 m) deep in a box column mold in any seventy-two-hour period. No more than a depth of 35 feet (11 m) of concrete could be poured into any mold over a thirty-day period. Because Six Companies had already raced through the greater part of the job, the Bureau of Reclamation sent one of its top men, Walker Young, to make sure the company slowed down on this part of the project.

Under normal circumstances, Young and Crowe liked each other. They'd known each other for twenty years and had worked on other dams together. But the two squabbled constantly about pouring the concrete for Hoover Dam. Crowe referred to Young as the Great Delayer, and Young referred to Crowe as Hurry Up.

With Hoover Dam finally going up, more newspaper reporters came to report on its progress. The feud between Walker and Crowe certainly spiced up their reports, although Walker admitted to one reporter, "Sometimes we fight with each other for the fun of it."

Whether it was fun or not, Walker held his ground. The concrete pouring proceeded slowly, based on contract terms and what the embedded thermometers revealed.

BUCKETS IN THE SKY

Pouring the concrete was one of the easiest and one of the hardest parts of the job. The easy part was simply pouring concrete into a series of box molds and waiting for it to harden. The hard part was that a lot was going on in a very small space. The dam would be nearly 800 feet (244 m) high, and Black Canyon was extremely narrow.

As Frank Crowe put it, "We had 5,000 men in a 4,000-foot [1,220 m] canyon. The problem, which was a problem in materials flow, was to set up the right sequence of jobs so [the workers] wouldn't kill each other off."

Concrete was the material that needed to flow. Mixing it was easy enough. High Mix was now running at full capacity. But getting it poured into the correct mold was difficult. To solve the problem, Crowe devised an aerial tramway system.

Crowe's tram system consisted of ten aerial towers that spanned the canyon. Each tower was 90 feet (27 m) tall, had wheels on its base, and

> "We had 5,000 men in a 4,000-foot [1,220 m] canyon. The problem. . . . was to set up the right sequence of jobs so [the workers] wouldn't kill each other off."
>
> **—Frank Crowe**

Workers finish construction of tramway towers.

Left, a worker monitors the central gauges for the tramway cables. Operating the tram system was solitary work. *Right,* workers steady a bucket of concrete.

was set on railroad tracks. This allowed the towers to move back and forth in the canyon. A complex network of steel cables connected all the towers to the concrete-mixing facilities and to all sections of the dam. By hooking giant buckets to the cable system, concrete could be delivered anywhere in the canyon.

The entire tram system was controlled by a cable operator sitting in a tiny shack, perched on a platform that extended 30 feet (9 m) into the canyon. He moved everything from this perch, based on hand signals received from signalmen at the bottom of the canyon. The operator could zoom an empty bucket over to High Mix, then send a loaded bucket of concrete back to the construction site. Buckets, each holding 8 cubic yards (6 m³) of concrete, swung through the canyon. They could deliver a massive quantity of concrete to where it was needed.

BURIED IN HOOVER DAM?

The cable system was efficient but dangerous. The stress of carrying heavy loads weakened the steel cables over time. They were constantly inspected for signs of wear, but a cable that looked perfectly fine could snap without warning.

One accident, which occurred during the overnight shift on January 3, 1935, involved a terrible death and an amazing escape. Two workers, Ike Johnson and J. W. "Happy" Pitts, were standing in a mold, waiting

for a bucket of concrete to arrive. Pitts was hunched down over a cooling pipe, checking its placement. Johnson was giving hand signals for the proper delivery of the bucket.

The enormous bucket, fully loaded with concrete, swung downward, coming in perfectly over the mold. Just as it twitched to a stop, one of the hoist cables snapped without warning. The bucket began to swing like a pendulum, first sweeping across the form, then out over the face of the dam, gathering speed as it went.

DEATH IN ARIZONA... OR NEVADA?

Hoover Dam straddled the Arizona-Nevada border. The dividing line between the states was down the middle of Black Canyon. Normally this was irrelevant, but the line became important when someone was killed at the site.

Whenever a worker was killed, the state in which the death occurred paid death benefits to his survivors. Arizona's benefits were higher than Nevada's, so if someone was killed in the canyon, his coworkers usually moved the body to the Arizona side. Medical benefits also were better in Arizona, so injured workers tried to crawl to the Arizona side, too.

Six Companies had to contribute to the compensation funds of both states. At one point, Six Companies tried to stop paying the Arizona compensation fund because the costs were so high. The company considered it unfair that workers never seemed to get injured or die on the Nevada side.

Both Johnson and Pitts were hit by the swinging bucket. Workers watched in horror as Pitts sailed over the side of the form and crashed in a lifeless heap 150 feet (46 m) below in the bottom of the canyon. The rampaging bucket next ricocheted off the dam face, dumped its load of concrete, and smashed into the Nevada side of the canyon. It shattered with a tremendous explosion.

Workers scrambled into the canyon, searching frantically for Johnson. He was nowhere to be found. Suddenly someone noticed a tiny flicker of light high on the face of the dam. Scurrying up ladders and catwalks (narrow walkways), they hurried to the light.

It was Johnson, covered with concrete, but fully conscious and frantically lighting matches to attract attention. The bucket had struck him behind the knees and scooped him up as it swung. Three-quarters of the way across the dam, the bucket had emptied its contents, depositing him and the concrete on the dam's face. Amazingly, he had ended up on one of the catwalks.

One worker came even closer to being buried in the dam. On another overnight shift, the sides of a freshly filled form gave way. The entire mass of wet concrete cascaded down a slot in the face of the dam that was used for ladders and catwalks. W. A. Jameson, a worker on a catwalk in the slot, was caught in the avalanche. He was swept 100 feet (30 m) to his death. When the slide finally stopped, there was no trace of Jameson, only an enormous pile of wet concrete studded with timber and other debris.

At 3:30 A.M., workers began the gruesome task of retrieving his body. They completed the job at 7:30 P.M. the next evening. Although accidents continued to occur, Jameson was the only worker who ever came close to being buried in the dam.

THE GAS CASES

By the fall of 1933, work on Hoover Dam was going smoothly. A magnificent structure was rising from the bottom of a desolate canyon in the Nevada desert. Everything seemed to be going perfectly for Six Companies.

Trouble was on the horizon, though. On October 17, the first of the carbon monoxide lawsuits against Six Companies, referred to as "the gas cases," went to trial in Las Vegas. With its victory over the Nevada mining laws in 1931, the company had considered the matter of toxic tunnels closed. But the affected workers had not. Dozens of them had hired lawyers to file suits against Six Companies.

Six Companies fought the cases vigorously for more than two years. But as each case came to trial, the company was shown to have willfully ignored mining laws. Workers' lawyers also presented evidence that the operation of gasoline-powered vehicles in a closed space is lethal.

Six Companies was also shown to have engaged in a criminal conspiracy to control the outcome of the first trials by intimidating witnesses and paying off jury members. For most of the Hoover Dam project, Six Companies had been seen by the general public as a compassionate, public-spirited company. The gas cases changed that. From then on, nearly everything Six Companies did became suspect.

On August 6, 1935, the *Las Vegas Evening Review-Journal* reported that forty-eight gas cases were pending against the company. They were seeking a combined total of $4.8 million in damages. In January 1936, Six Companies reached an out-of-court settlement with the workers.

The amount Six Companies paid was never disclosed. If the company's legal fees, the expenses incurred in bribes to fix the trials, and the actual payments to settle the lawsuits were added together, the settlement amount was most certainly more than $300,000. This is the amount it would have cost Six Companies to convert the tunnel trucks to electricity. Their damaged reputation was yet another cost of the gas cases.

Long after everyone knew the dam would be done early, work continued around the clock.

PENSTOCKS, INTAKE TOWERS, AND GENERATORS

The gas cases made for interesting reading across the nation. But it was business as usual in Black Canyon. Work proceeded at a furious clip.

In March 1934, the last concrete was poured for the tunnels. By June 1, 1934, the dam was two-thirds complete. On July 20, 1934, Six Companies employed a record number of people: 5,251.

On December 5, 1934, the 3 millionth cubic yard (2.3 millionth m³) of concrete was poured in the dam. Newspapers noted that one day past the contract's original start date for cement pouring, the dam was already 92 percent complete. Only sixty-three days later, the first column in the dam reached its final height of 726 feet (221 m). By the time Hoover Dam reached its full height, enough concrete had been poured into the structure to pave a two-lane highway from Los Angeles to New York.

As the dam neared its final height, other aspects of the project were also nearing completion. Part of the contract called for Six Companies to build four intake towers. These would take the water from the reservoir behind the dam and deliver it to a powerhouse at the base of the dam. The water would flow through penstocks, or enormous pipes, between the towers and the powerhouse. The force of the water flowing through the penstocks would power the generators to produce electricity for the region.

Six Companies blasted the tunnels for the penstocks. The government had hired another company, Babcock & Wilcox, of Ohio, to build the penstocks. Each section of penstock was 30 feet (9 m) in diameter and weighed 170 tons (154 metric tons). Because of this massive size, there was no way to transport the sections from Ohio. Babcock & Wilcox had to build a steel fabrication plant at the site. To get the monstrous pieces of pipe from the plant and into the tunnels, the government built its own cable system, modeled on the one Frank Crowe had designed.

Construction on the intake towers had progressed along with the dam. By the end of 1934, all four of the 395-foot (120-m) towers were more than halfway finished. The powerhouse that would generate electricity was almost complete by the end of 1934. Six Companies only needed to build the basic structure. The government would finish it, install the generators, and operate the power plant.

Catwalks and scaffolding connect the rising intake towers on the Nevada side of the river.

MORE VISITORS, FEWER WORKERS

Besides being a record year for employment at the dam, 1934 was also a record year for tourism. That year 266,436 visitors checked in to see Boulder City and the dam. The Union Pacific Railroad ran weekly excursion trains to the site. The Boulder Dam Hotel was booked solid.

Tourism continued to increase as the number of workers dropped off. Hoover Dam was almost finished. Workers were leaving and moving on to other projects. Six Companies had already won the bid to build Parker Dam, the second dam in Arthur Powell Davis's envisioned network of dams for the Colorado River. Many of the workers moved on to that project. By 1934 Frank Crowe was already spending most of his time at Parker Dam.

On November 3, 1934, Low Mix produced its last cubic yard of concrete. It shut down after more than two years of continuous operation. The plant was broken down and reassembled at Parker Dam. For nearly four years, the Boulder Canyon project had riveted the nation. Finally, it was drawing to a close.

Chapter Seven
TAMING THE COLORADO?
(1935–modern times)

J ANUARY 31, 1935, WAS THE last day of freedom for the Colorado River. The next morning, a giant control gate slammed shut in Tunnel No. 4. This forced the river into Tunnel No. 1, where a network of opening and closing valves controlled its passage. Enough water was sent down Black Canyon to irrigate the Imperial Valley. The rest was blocked to begin forming a reservoir behind the dam.

"GEE, THIS IS MAGNIFICENT!"
Boulder City buzzed with activity on the morning of September 30, 1935. People hurried through the streets, dressed in their best. On the highway from Las Vegas, cars inched forward bumper to bumper. Eventually more than twelve thousand people lined the rim of the canyon and the road on the top of the dam. Hoover Dam was officially finished. The president of the United States was coming to dedicate it.

Above, a crowd filled the Hoover Dam powerhouse to witness the generator in the foreground go to work. It would generate the first electricity to come from Hoover Dam. *Right,* President Franklin D. Roosevelt dedicated the dam.

At 10:30 A.M., a motorcade pulled up to the dam, and President Franklin D. Roosevelt stepped from the first car. Looking around him at the giant structure and the milling crowds, Roosevelt's face broke into a broad smile. "Gee, this is magnificent," he exclaimed.

Nearly every one of the five hundred workers who still remained on the project had come to hear Roosevelt's dedication of the dam. For them Roosevelt's opening remarks struck a special chord as he said:

> Ten years ago the place where we are gathered was an unpeopled, forbidding desert. In the bottom of a gloomy canyon, whose precipitous wall rose to a height of more than one thousand feet [300 m], flowed a turbulent, dangerous river. The mountains on either side were difficult of access, with neither road nor rail, and their rocks were protected by neither trees nor grass from the blazing heat of the sun. The site of Boulder City was a cactus-covered waste. The transformation wrought here is a twentieth-century marvel.

As the president continued, the workers looked around. They saw reminders everywhere of just how hard the job had been. Over there a high scaler had fallen to his death. Near the middle of the dam was the place where Jameson had been buried in a concrete avalanche.

THE LAST DEATH

The last person to die on the project made even confirmed skeptics believe in fate. On December 20, 1922, J. G. Tierney, a driller on the Bureau of Reclamation's original survey crew, had been swept off a barge and drowned in the Colorado River. Exactly thirteen years later, on December 20, 1935, his son, Patrick Tierney, a twenty-five-year-old electrician's helper, slipped while working on an intake tower and fell 325 feet (99 m) to his death.

Young Tierney was the last of ninety-six workers on the government's official death list. Of these, twenty-six were struck by falling debris, twenty-six were struck by machinery or heavy equipment, twenty-four fell to their deaths, ten were killed in explosions, five were electrocuted, three drowned, one died in a cable accident, and one died in an elevator accident. The many workers who died from heat stroke, carbon monoxide poisoning, or other work-related illnesses were never recorded in the official death total.

Under the president's feet was the tunnel where other workers had been killed in a rock slide.

But the workers also realized what they had accomplished. Roosevelt concluded by saying, "I have the right once more to congratulate you who have created Boulder Dam and on behalf of the nation to say to you, 'Well done.'" Thunderous applause erupted in the canyon. The dam was built, and it was magnificent.

WHAT NEXT?

On February 29, 1936, Frank Crowe stood on the crest of Hoover Dam surrounded by reporters. Flashbulbs popped as he announced to government representatives, "As representative of Six Companies, Inc., builders of this dam, I am very happy to turn over the job for your acceptance."

The next day, in Washington, D. C., the government formally signed off on its contract with Six Companies. The dam had been completed two years, one month, and twenty-eight days ahead of schedule. Six Companies had put everything on the line to have a chance to build the largest dam in the world. The gamble had paid of, and the job was done.

When all the expenses were paid, Six Companies was left with between $10.4 and $18 million in profit, which was distributed among the owners of the companies. All went on to continued financial success. They never built another gigantic dam together, but all members of the partnership remained friends and sometimes worked on other projects together.

Hoover Dam had made Frank Crowe a wealthy man. In addition to his salary of $18,000 a year, he had also received 2.5 percent of the profits. He finished Parker Dam ahead of schedule, then supervised the construction of several other dams. Since he loved building dams, he had no intention of retiring with his wealth. As he told a reporter two days after turning Hoover Dam over to the government, "I'm looking for a job and want to go right on building dams as long as I live."

Crowe didn't need to worry about work. He was always in demand among dam builders. Pacific Constructors hired him as the general superintendent for construction of Shasta Dam in northern California, a dam that rivaled Hoover in size and complexity. When it was finished in 1944, Crowe was sixty-two years old. He had been doing hard labor for most of his life.

In 1945, with the end of World War II, the U.S. government asked him to organize and direct all the reconstruction work for the U.S. Zone of Occupation in Germany. He wanted to accept the job, but his doctor advised him not to. Frank Crowe reluctantly retired to a cattle ranch he owned near Shasta Dam. He died there on February 26, 1946.

ARCHITECTS, ARTISTS, AND HOOVER DAM

The original design for Hoover Dam was much fussier than the one visitors see. For example, it called for a row of giant eagles atop the crest of the dam. The U.S. Bureau of Reclamation hired Gordon Kaufmann, an English architect working in Los Angeles, to help with the final design. Kaufmann wiped away all embellishments. He felt the dam was a powerful statement by itself.

Decoration would only take away from its beauty. His one concession was to place narrow vertical ridges at the top edge of the dam's face. Barely noticeable on their own, the protrusions create an interesting pattern of shadows, *left,* as the sun moves across the sky.

Allen True, Kaufmann's assistant, was responsible for the Native American motifs, *near right,* in the power plants' terrazzo (marble chips set in cement) floors.

Oskar J. W. Hansen, a Norwegian-born naturalized citizen, created the large winged figures *(far right, top)* on either side of the flag on the Nevada side of the dam. Hansen wanted the figures to reflect the grandeur of the dam and the courage of the men who built it. He also created the star map in front of the flag that tells

future generations exactly when the dam was dedicated.

In 1995 Steven Ligouri, a local sculptor, and Bert Hansen, the owner of the Hoover Dam snack bar, created a bronze statue to honor the high scalers who had worked on the dam, *below*. Ligouri modeled the sculpture after Joe Kline, one of the last surviving high scalers. Ligouri presented Kline with a 2-foot (0.6 m) version of the sculpture on September 30, 1995, the sixtieth anniversary of Hoover Dam.

Ligouri and Hansen then created a much larger version of the same statue. In 2000, the larger-than-life statue was installed in front of the visitor's center and dedicated to all the high scalers who had worked on Hoover Dam. A dam worker placed a flag in the high scaler's hand following terrorist attacks in New York City and Washington, D.C., on September 11, 2001.

Water that the Hoover Dam diverts to Yolo County, California, waters these rice paddies.

A BLOOMING DESERT

The completion of Hoover Dam marked the opening of the West for modern development. The dam supplied enormous amounts of power and water to an area that had previously had neither.

Between 1936 and 1939, nine turbine generators were installed in the powerhouse at Hoover Dam. Four more generators were installed during World War II (1939–1945), three more generators in 1952, and one more in 1961. A total of seventeen generators were in operation in 2002, eight on the Arizona side and nine on the Nevada side.

The sale of this power was always intended to pay back the $200 million in congressional appropriations for the Boulder Dam Project. In 1986, the final payment—with interest—was made.

The power generated by the dam fueled the growth of Los Angeles, Phoenix, Las Vegas, and other towns in the Southwest. The All-American Canal, carrying water from the Colorado River, opened in 1940. With it, Southern California became a blooming agricultural oasis. Thanks to Hoover, and other dams, California produces more food for the United States than any other state in the union.

The aerospace industry in southern California was just getting its start in the early 1940s. With the coming of World War II, the industry boomed with the power supplied by Hoover Dam. It continues to be a vital part of California's and the United States' economy.

BOULDER CITY

When the Hoover Dam project ended, few people expected Boulder City or Las Vegas to survive. As workers moved out of Boulder City, its population declined and businesses closed. By 1940 only twenty-six hundred people remained there.

The city also shrank physically because Utah Construction had a separate deal with Six Companies to sell many of the buildings in the town for scrap. Hundreds of cottages, six dormitories, the recreation hall, and the mess hall were torn down and sold.

Boulder City probably would have faded into oblivion had it not been for World War II. A magnesium plant opened in nearby Henderson, Nevada. A lack of housing there forced plant workers into Boulder City. The army also quartered troops in the town to guard the dam from possible Japanese attack. Gradually, Boulder City began to grow again.

In 1960 the town was declared independent of the U.S. government, ending thirty years of federal administration. Although free to run itself, the town continued to ban alcohol until 1969. It remains the only town in Nevada where gambling is prohibited.

Gradually, too, Boulder City began to prosper. The town's lawns grew lush, and the trees that Wilbur Weed planted grew up. People flocked to Boulder City in such numbers that the town had to pass an ordinance in 1979 to limit further growth.

HOOVER DAM PASSES THE TEST

Although supplying power to the region was important, Hoover Dam was built primarily to control the Colorado River. In many years, the river flows smoothly along its course. But in other years, without warning, heavy rains or melting snow might start a flood that could wipe out everything in its path.

While the reservoir—named Lake Mead—was filling up, the danger of flooding was minimal. When floodwater roared into the far end of the reservoir, the expanse of the lake could contain it. By the time it reached the dam, it was little more than a rough ripple.

The original diversion tunnels still have a job to do. When Lake Mead threatens to overflow its banks, excess water can be channeled through the tunnels and into the Colorado River below the dam.

In 1983, however, the reservoir was filled. In late spring, snowstorms in the Rocky Mountains were followed by a heat wave and heavy rainstorms. Between April and July, the runoff into the Colorado River was 210 percent above normal, and every reservoir in the system was filled to capacity. On June 6, 1983, Lake Mead was so full that dam officials had to make small emergency releases of water into the canyon.

But water kept pouring into Lake Mead. By July more than 90,000 cubic feet (2,500 m³) of water per second was pouring into the reservoir. On July 2, 1983, officials lifted the dam's gigantic steel gates for the first time. An enormous wave of water surged into the spillway channels and poured into the diversion tunnels. As the water hit the canyon, a huge cloud of mist rose in the hot desert air. The water raced down Black Canyon, roaring like a freight train as it headed toward the Imperial Valley.

Hoover Dam's gates stayed open until September 6, 1983. Flood damage was substantial all along the Colorado, but it was only a fraction of the damage that would have occurred without Hoover Dam and the easing effect of Lake Mead.

The flood of 1983 also demonstrated just how well Hoover Dam had been built. Other dams along the flood path suffered substantial damage to their diversion tunnels. At Glen Canyon Dam, built in the 1950s, the concrete pitted and broke away in the wash of floodwater. But when the water raced through the diversion tunnels at Hoover Dam, at speeds of 120 miles (193 km) per hour, Frank Crowe's concrete stayed intact. It suffered only minor pitting and abrading. Six Companies built it fast, but they built it well.

HOOVER DAM AND LAKE MEAD IN MODERN TIMES

Hoover Dam is no longer the tallest dam in the world. Rogun Dam in Russia is 374 feet (114 m) higher. But Hoover Dam is still the most famous. Nearly one million people visit it each year. They walk along its crest and visit its tourist center.

In 1984 Lake Mead was formally named the Lake Mead National Recreation Area. The lake, when full, holds enough water to cover the state of New York to a depth of 1 foot (0.3 m). Just as some engineers had predicted, the weight of the water in Lake Mead caused some earthquakes, but they have all been small. None of them has disturbed the dam or the millions of people who use the lake each year.

> "There's something peculiarly satisfying about building a dam. You know what you build will stand for centuries."
>
> —**Frank Crowe**

Modern visitors are just as impressed with Hoover Dam as the earliest tourists were. The pounding jackhammers are gone, the rumbling trucks have vanished, and the daring high scalers are just a memory. But the awe-inspiring magnificence of the dam remains.

Rising majestically from the bottom of a narrow canyon, the dam stands as a monument to those who built it. As Frank Crowe said in 1943, "There's something peculiarly satisfying about building a dam. You know what you build will stand for centuries." Nearing its first century, Hoover Dam is truly a great building feat.

A Timeline of the Hoover Dam

1540 Spanish conquistadors arrive at the Colorado River and explore its lower reaches.

1858 Lieutenant Joseph Ives navigates the Colorado in *The Explorer* and reaches the end of Black Canyon.

1869 John Wesley Powell makes the first recorded trip through the Grand Canyon

1901 The Imperial Valley Canal is built.

1905–1907 The Colorado River floods the Imperial Valley, causing extensive damage and creating the Salton Sea.

1918 Arthur Powell Davis, Bureau of Reclamation director and chief engineer, proposes control of the Colorado by a dam in Boulder Canyon.

1928 Boulder Canyon Project Act passes the U.S. Senate on December 14, the House of Representatives on December 18, and is signed by President Calvin Coolidge on December 21.

1929 Six of the seven states approve Colorado River Compact. Boulder Canyon Project Act declared effective June 25.

1931 Bureau of Reclamation awards contract to Six Companies March 11. Construction begins in Black Canyon.

1932 River is diverted around the dam site November 14.

1933 First concrete is poured in dam June 6.

1935 Dam starts holding back water in Lake Mead on February 1. Last concrete is placed in dam on May 29. President Franklin D. Roosevelt dedicates dam on September 30.

1938 Lake Mead extends 110 miles (176 km) upstream. Generators N-5 and N-6 begin operation on June 26 and August 31.

1947 Eightieth Congress passes legislation officially designating the Boulder Canyon Project's key structure as "Hoover Dam" in honor of President Herbert Hoover.

1985 Hoover Dam celebrates its fiftieth anniversary. Most of the cost of the Boulder Canyon project has been repaid to the Federal Treasury.

2002 One hundredth anniversary of the Bureau of Reclamation celebrated at Hoover Dam.

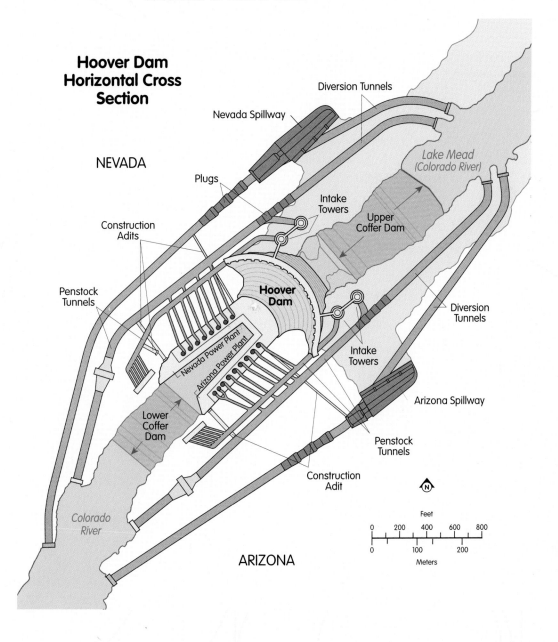

**Hoover Dam
Horizontal Cross
Section**

44444444444

Source Notes

Acknowledgments for quoted material: pp.11, 13, 20, 29, 32, 35, 39, 42, 51, 54, 55, 60, 66, 72, 73, 81, 82, 83, and 89 Joseph E. Stevens, *Hoover Dam: An American Adventure* (Norman, OK: University of Oklahoma Press, 1988).

Selected Bibliography

Dunbar, Andrew J., and Dennis McBride. *Building Hoover Dam: An Oral History of the Great Depression*. Reno, NV: University of Nevada Press, 1993.

Gusmorino, Paul A., III. "Main Causes of the Great Depression." *Gusmorino World* (May 13, 1996).
<http://www.escape.com/~paulg53/politics/great_depression.shtml>

KC Publications. *Construction of Hoover Dam: A Historic Account Prepared in Cooperation with the Department of the Interior, Bureau of Reclamation*. Las Vegas, NV: KC Publications, 1976.

———. *The Story Behind Hoover Dam*. Las Vegas, NV: KC Publications, 1931–1935.

Maxon, James C. *Lake Mead & Hoover Dam: The Story behind the Scenery*. Las Vegas, NV: KC Publications, 1980.

Rhinehart, Julian. "The Grand Dam." *Nevada Magazine* (October, 1995).

Simonds, William Joe. *The Boulder Canyon Project: Hoover Dam*. N.d.
<http://www.usbr.gov./history/hoover.htm>

Stevens, Joseph E. *Hoover Dam: An American Adventure*. Norman, OK: University of Oklahoma Press, 1988.

U.S. Department of the Interior, Bureau of Reclamation. *High Scaler Monument*. N.d. <http://www.hooverdam.usbr.gov/service/newstatu.html>

———. *Hoover Dam. National Historic Landmark*. N.d.
<http://www.hooverdam.usbr.gov/service/index.html>

———. *Hoover Dam Sculptures and Star Map*. N.d.
<http://www.hooverdam.usbr.gov/service/sculptur.html>

Wolf, Donald E., et al. *Big Dams and Other Dreams: The Six Companies Story*. Norman, OK: The University of Oklahoma Press, 1996.

Woodbury, Chuck, ed. "U.S. Camel Corps Remembered in Quartzite, Arizona." *Out West.* N.d.<http://www.outwestnewspaper.com/camels.html>

Further Reading and Websites

Damon, Duane. *Headin' for Better Times: The Arts of the Great Depression.* Minneapolis: Lerner Publications Company, 2002.
Learn about the great art and cultural feats of the same period in which the Hoover Dam was built. The painters, photographers, poets, actors, and other artists of the Great Depression both reflected and shaped America's view of itself for decades to come.

Kelly, James E., and William R. Park. *The Dam Builders.* Reading, MA: Addison-Wesley Publishing Company, Inc., 1977.
This book traces each step in dam construction and includes detailed descriptions of the machinery and equipment used.

Mann, Elizabeth. *The Hoover Dam: The Story of Hard Times, Tough People, and the Taming of a Wild River.* New York: Mikaya Press, 2001.
Readers will find a wealth of information about construction of the Hoover Dam. Readers will discover how hard hats were invented, hear the voices of the dam builders themselves, and view fantastic pictures of dam construction.

PBS. *Building Big: Dams.*
<http://www.pbs.org/wgbh/buildingbig/dam/index.html>
Learn the ins and outs of all different types of dams at this extensive site. Compare the Hoover Dam with other famous dams, view pictures, and take the "Dam Challenge" to decide what should be done to fix dam problems.

Rawlins, Carol B. *The Colorado River.* New York: Franklin Watts, 1999.
This book documents both the history of the Colorado River and its present-day uses from recreation to hydroelectric power.

U.S. Department of the Interior, Bureau of Reclamation. *Hoover Dam Sculptures and Star Map.*
<http://www.hooverdam.usbr.gov/service/sculptur.html>
This website contains both photos and explanations of the art of the Hoover Dam for a better understanding of "The Winged Figures of the Republic," the bas-reliefs (carvings) on the elevator towers, and the star map.

Index

adit tunnels, 42–44, 52

African Americans, 62

All-American Canal Bill, 18

Anderson Brothers, 61

arched-gravity design, 22–23

architecture, 58, 84

Arizona, 10, 16, 24, 26, 76

Black Canyon, 5, 7, 8, 11, 12, 20–21, 34, 40, 69, 76

Boulder Canyon, 20–21, 22

Boulder City, 26, 58–62, 64, 79, 80, 87

California, 10, 16, 19, 26

canyon walls, 19, 20–21, 23, 36–37, 41, 47–48, 62, 68

carbon monoxide poisoning, 7, 49, 77

cofferdams, 25, 41, 66–69

Colorado, 8, 26

Colorado River, 5, 7, 8–17; canal on, 14–17, 18, 86; control of, 7, 18, 79; currents, 10, 21, 23, 36, 51; dams on, 79; explorations of, 7, 10–13; map, 6; moving of, 40–41, 54–55, 67

Colorado River Compact, 26

concrete, 23, 24, 53–54, 62, 66, 70–76, 78; box forms for, 69, 70, 72; drying, 70–71; mixing facilities, 24, 56, 65, 66, 79

Coolidge, Calvin, 57

Cowan, Oliver, 48–49

Crowe, Frank, 29, 30–32, 39, 44, 45, 49, 50, 51, 54, 58, 66, 69, 70–73, 82–83, 89

Davis, Arthur Powell, 17–18, 20, 22, 32, 79

deaths, 7, 21, 38–39, 49, 74–77, 81, 83

DeBoer, S. R., 58

debris, clearing of, 21, 37, 43, 45, 46, 50, 53, 69

desert, 7, 9, 14, 17, 18, 56

diversion tunnels, 24, 40–41, 42–44, 53–55, 56, 62, 66, 69, 88

dynamite and dynamiting, 36–37, 38–39, 40, 44–45, 46

electricity, 7, 19, 25, 36, 48, 49, 78, 80, 86

equipment, 19, 36, 38, 43, 45, 49, 54, 65, 67

Explorer, The, 11

Falls-Davis Report, 20

farms and farming, 14, 15, 86

floods, 7, 14, 15, 17, 51–53, 68, 87–89

gas cases, 77–78

gold, 13, 69

Grand Canyon, 8, 12

gravel, 23, 24, 62–63; gravel-processing plant, 24, 56, 62, 63, 65, 66, 69

Great Depression, 27, 32–33, 49, 59

Green River, 12, 13

Harding, Warren, 26

Harriman, Edward H., 16–17

hazards, 7, 38–39, 47, 49, 51, 56, 73, 83

Hoover, Herbert, 22, 26, 33, 35, 57

Hoover Dam: accidents, 38–39, 49, 64, 65–66, 74–77; bidding for, 26–29; choosing site for, 18–21; construction materials used in, 23, 36, 62, 66; cost and funding of, 19, 20, 26, 27, 33, 42, 63, 77, 86; design plans of, 22–25, 41, 66, 78–79, 84; dimensions of, 23–26, 32, 44, 78–79; name of, 22; natural obstacles to building of, 20–21, 32, 66; opening of, 80–81; reasons for, 18, 58, 87; timeline for building, 27, 35, 38, 42, 47, 56, 69, 70, 82 hydroelectric power. *See* electricity

Imperial Valley, California, 14–15, 17, 80
intake towers, 24, 25, 78–79
irrigation, 9, 14, 80
Ives, Joseph, 11, 13

Kaufmann, Gordon, 84
Kline, Joe, 85

labor strikes, 51
Las Vegas, Nevada, 7, 26, 30, 32, 35, 57,
    60, 77, 87
living conditions, 7, 34–36, 51, 56,
    59–61, 62

maps and diagrams, 6, 23, 24, 25, 43, 91
McKeever, Michael, 35
McKeeversville, 35
Mead, Elwood, 42
Mead, Lake, 83, 87, 88
Morrison-Knudsen, 27–28, 32
muck. *See* debris, clearing of

Native Americans, 9, 12, 14, 48, 84
Nevada, 24, 26, 60, 76; mining laws in,
    49
newspapers and journalists, 28, 29, 30,
    35, 62, 72, 78, 82

Parker Dam, 79, 83
Parks, Arnold, 48–49
penstocks, 78–79
Pitts, J. W. "Happy," 74–76
Powell, John Wesley, 11–13, 18
power station, 24, 25, 78–79, 80, 84
profits, 42, 82–83

Ragtown, 34–35, 58, 59
rail and road systems, 19, 26, 36, 37, 39,
    42, 65

reservoir, 19, 78, 80, 88
rock, 19, 20–21, 38, 39, 46–47
Roosevelt, Franklin D., 22, 33, 57,
    80–82
Roosevelt, Theodore, 16

safety miners, 47
Salton Sea, 15
Salton Sink, 14–15
Savage, Jack, 22
scalers, 47–49, 68, 69, 85
silt, 19, 20–21, 69
Six Companies, Incorporated, 32, 34, 41,
    49, 58, 61, 62, 66, 77, 78, 82, 89;
    founding of, 28–29; profits for, 82;
    and workers, 49–51, 64, 76, 78
Southern Pacific Railroad, 16–17
supplies, 19, 36, 38, 61

tourism, 8, 79, 83, 89
tram system, 73–74
tunnels. *See* diversion tunnels

unemployment, 27, 32–35
Union Pacific Railroad, 36, 79
U.S. Bureau of Reclamation, 17, 22,
    28–29, 35, 41, 60, 71, 84
U.S. Congress, 18, 20, 26
U.S. government, 10–11, 34, 60, 78–79,
    82, 83
Utah, 8, 26
Utah Construction, 27–28, 32, 87

Walter, Raymond, 22, 29
water needs, 7, 13–14, 26, 86. *See also*
    irrigation

Young, Walker, 29, 72

Lesley A. DuTemple has written more than a dozen books for young readers, including many award-winning titles such as her biography *Jacques Cousteau,* winner of the National Science Teachers Association/Children's Book Council Outstanding Science Trade Books for Children. After graduating from the University of California, San Diego, she attended the University of Utah's Graduate School of Architecture, where she concentrated in design and architectural history. The creator of the **Great Building Feats** series, she believes, "There's a human story behind every one of these building feats, and those stories are just as amazing as the projects themselves."

Photo Acknowledgments

The images in this book are used with the permission of: National Archives, Rocky Mountain Region pp. 1, 2–3, 21, 28–29, 38, 46 (bottom), 47, 48, 49, 50, 52, 53, 54, 55, 58–59, 60, 62, 63, 64 (bottom), 67, 69, 70, 70–71, 72, 73, 74, 75; Bureau of Reclamation, pp. 4, 20, 39, 58, 64 (top), 84 (center and bottom), 85 (top and bottom), 88; © A. A. M. Van der Heyden/Independent Picture Service, p. 4–5, 8–9; © Deborah C. Mink, p. 8; L. Maynard Dixon, Denver Public Library, Western History Department, p. 10; Utah State Historical Society, p. 12 (top and bottom); National Archives, pp. 13, 33; Library of Congress, pp. 14, 18–19, 22, 40–41, 78, 79; Pioneers Museum and Cultural Center of the Imperial Valley, pp. 15, 16–17; Photograph courtesy of Junior League of Las Vegas Collection, University of Nevada, Las Vegas Library, p. 30–31; Photograph courtesy of Virginia Fenton Collection, University of Nevada, Las Vegas Library, p. 32; Photograph courtesy of Elton & Madelaine Garret Collection, University of Nevada, Las Vegas Library, pp. 34, 51, 56; Kaiser Collection, Bancroft Library, pp. 37, 46 (top), 61, 68; Photograph courtesy of Union Pacific Railroad Collection, University of Nevada, Las Vegas Library, p. 56–7; Photo courtesy of W. A. Bechtel Collection, University of Nevada, Las Vegas, p. 65; AP/Wide World Photos, p. 80; Brown Studio, Huntington Park, California/courtesy of Franklin D. Roosevelt Library, p. 80–81; J.B. Cooke Collection, Bancroft Library, p. 83; © Buddy Mayes/Travel Stock, p. 84 (top); © George Lepp/AgStock USA, p. 86; Maps and diagrams by Laura Westlund, pp. 6, 23, 24, 25, 43, 45, 91.

Cover photos are by Library of Congress (front) and National Archives, Rocky Mountain Region (back).